Silent Night

A Greyscale colouring book

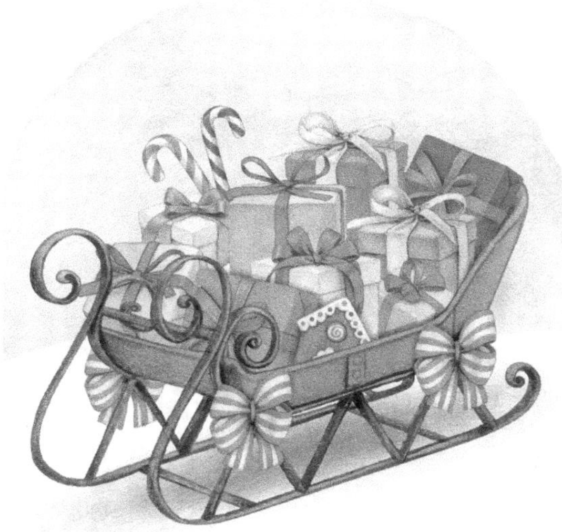

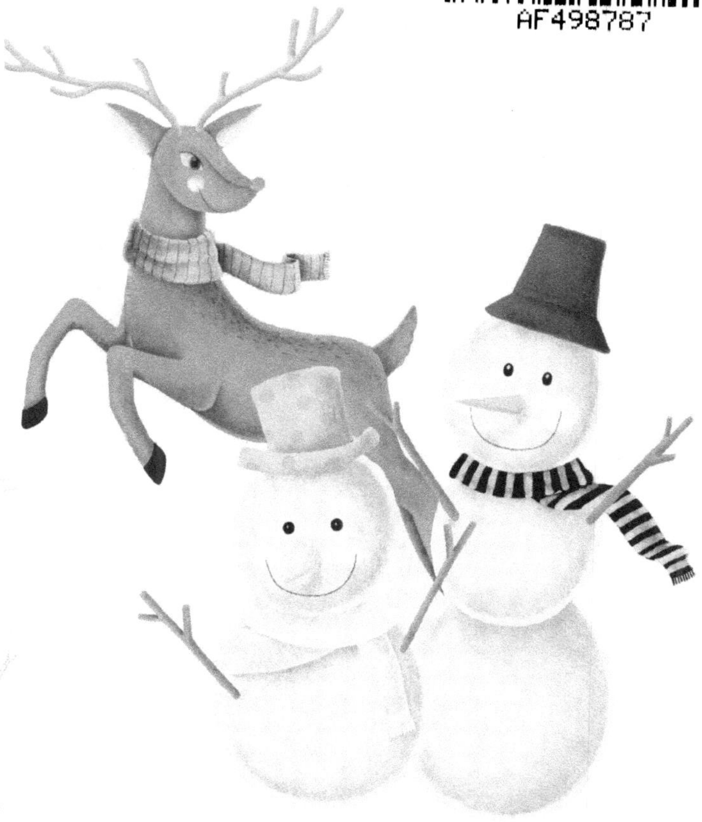

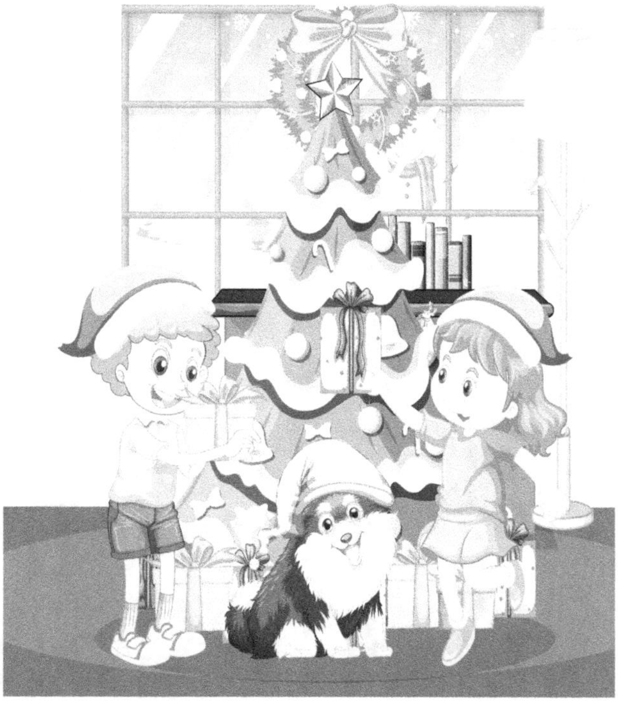

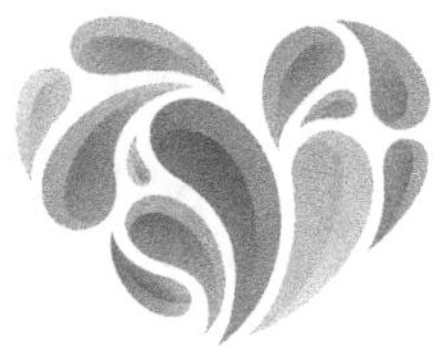

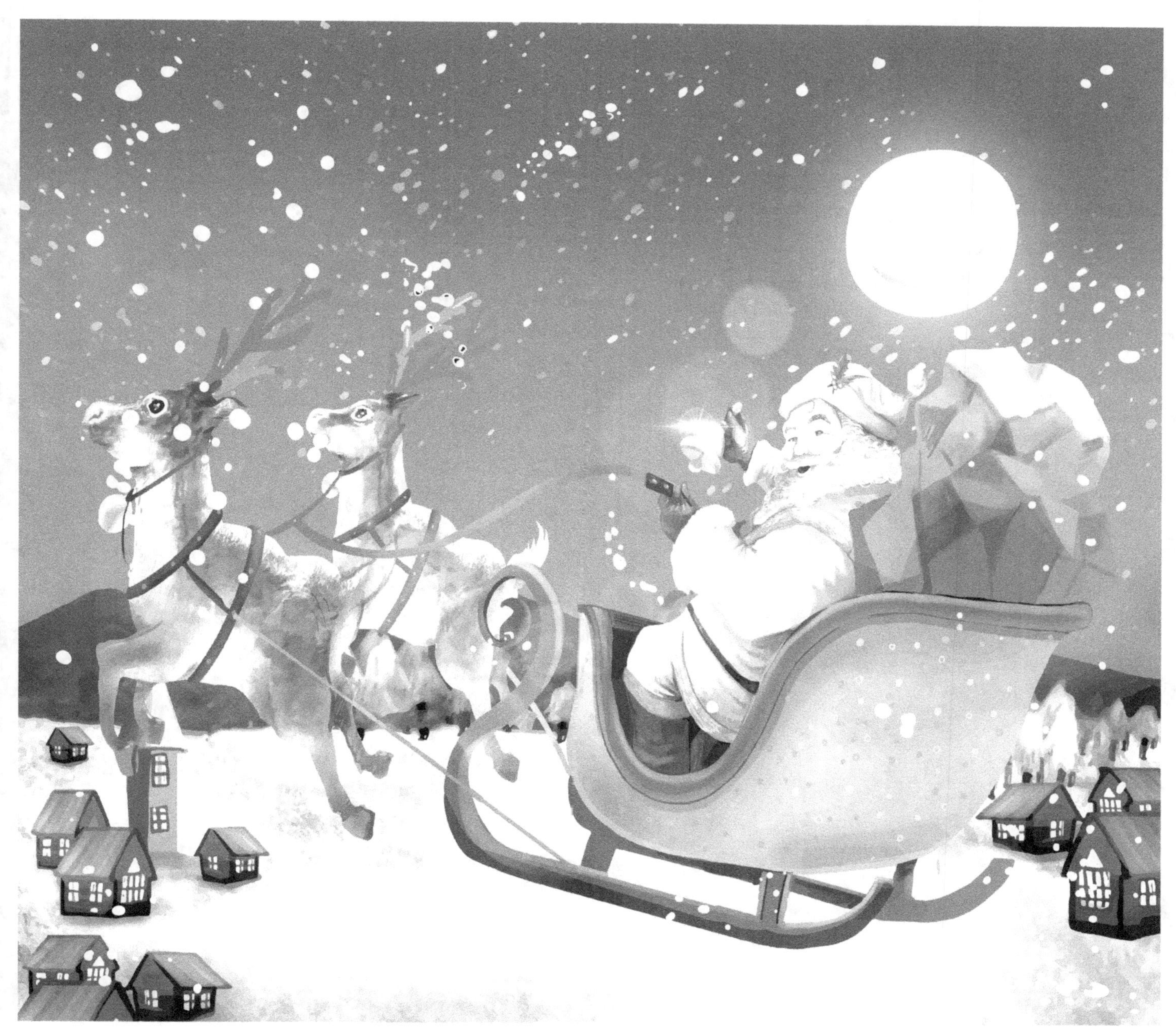

Silent Night

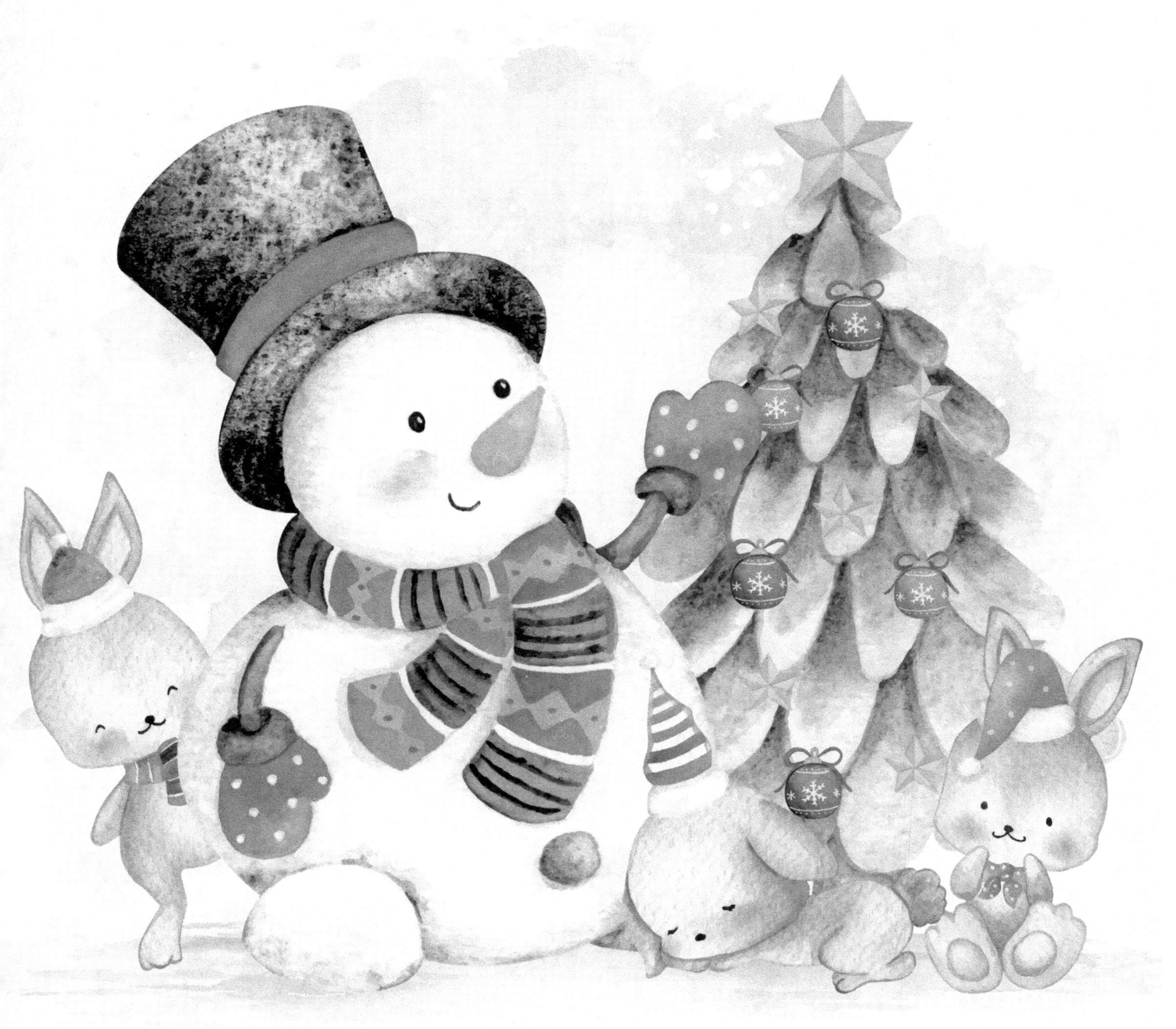

Christmas Time

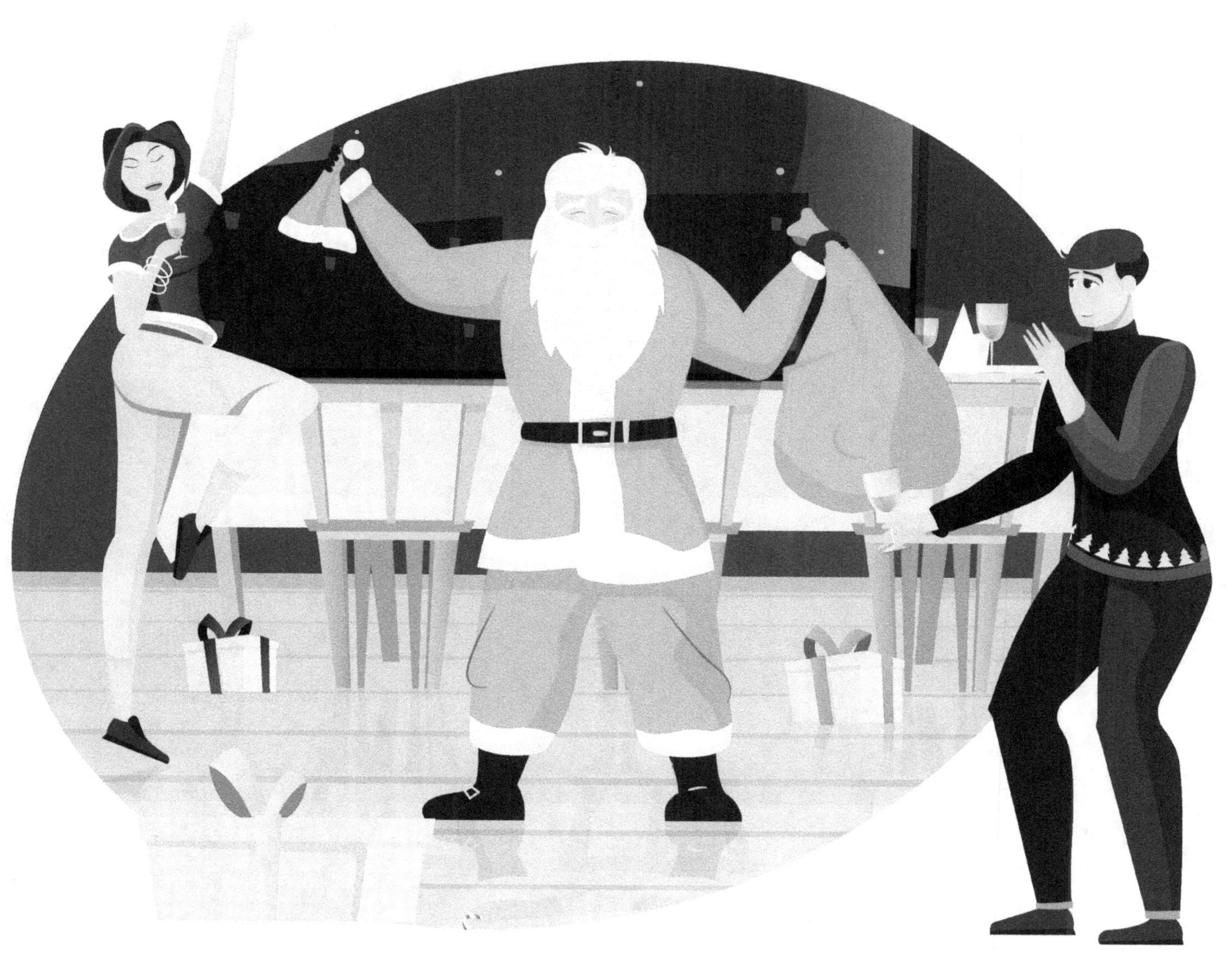

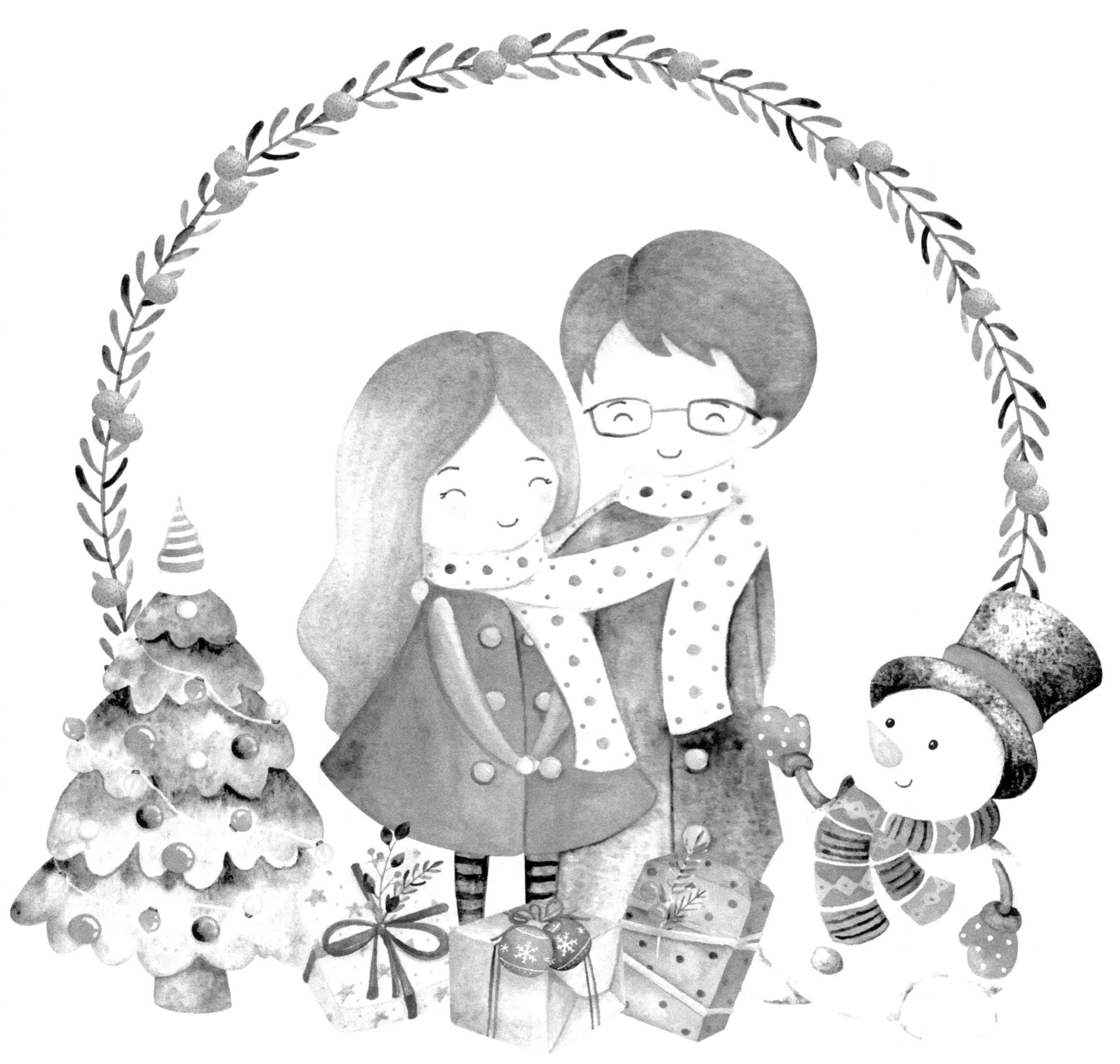

Joy

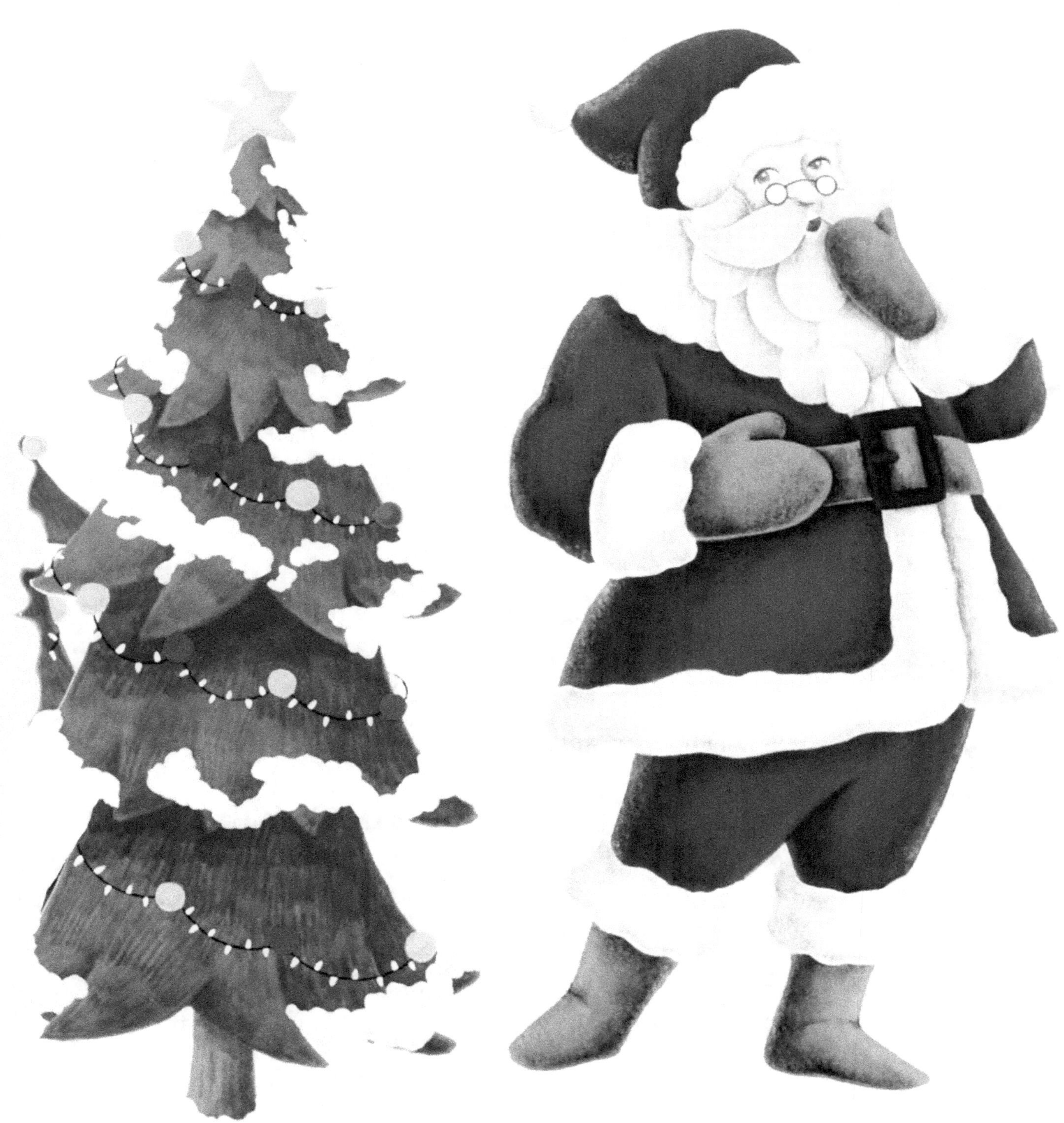

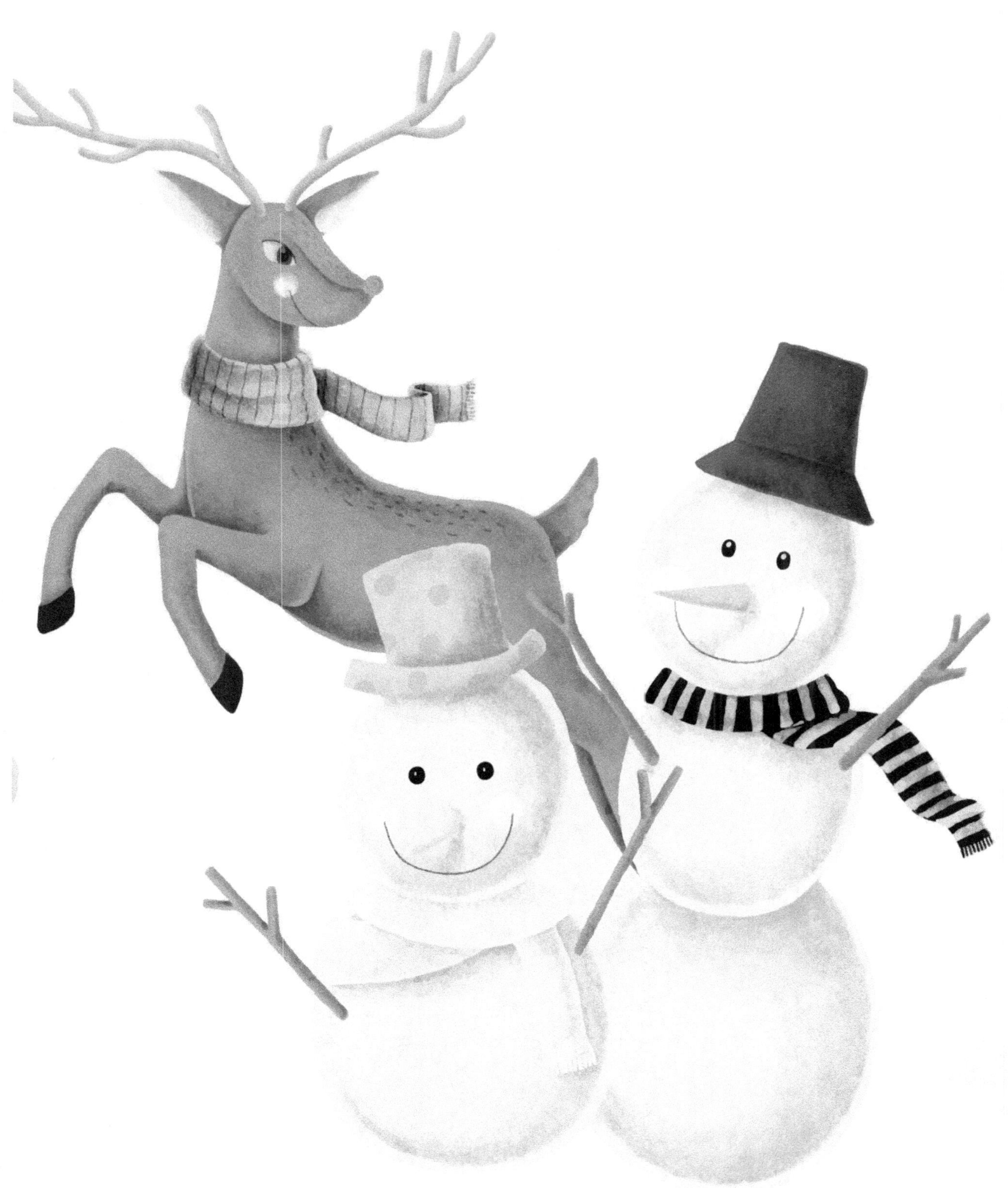

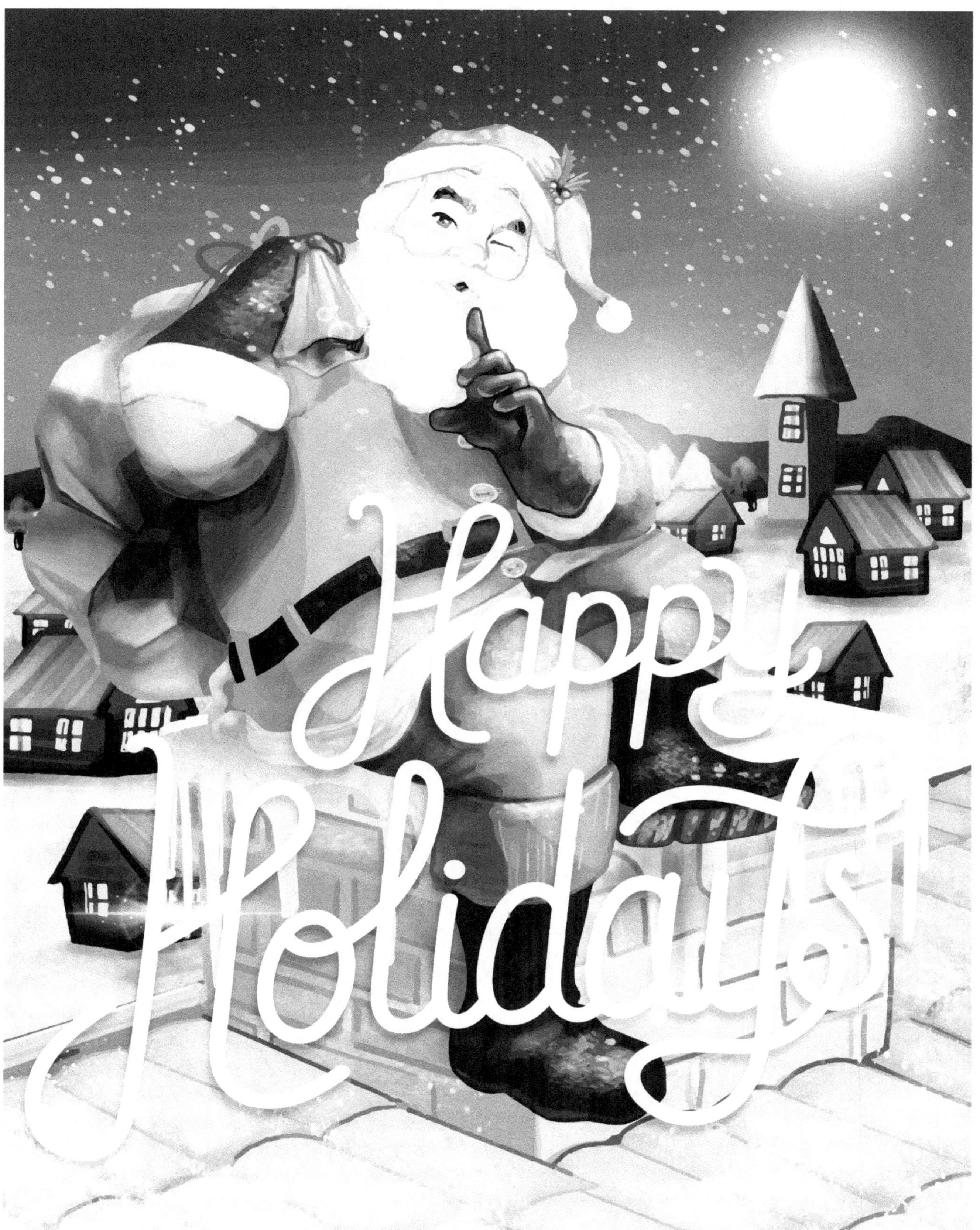

Happy Holidays!

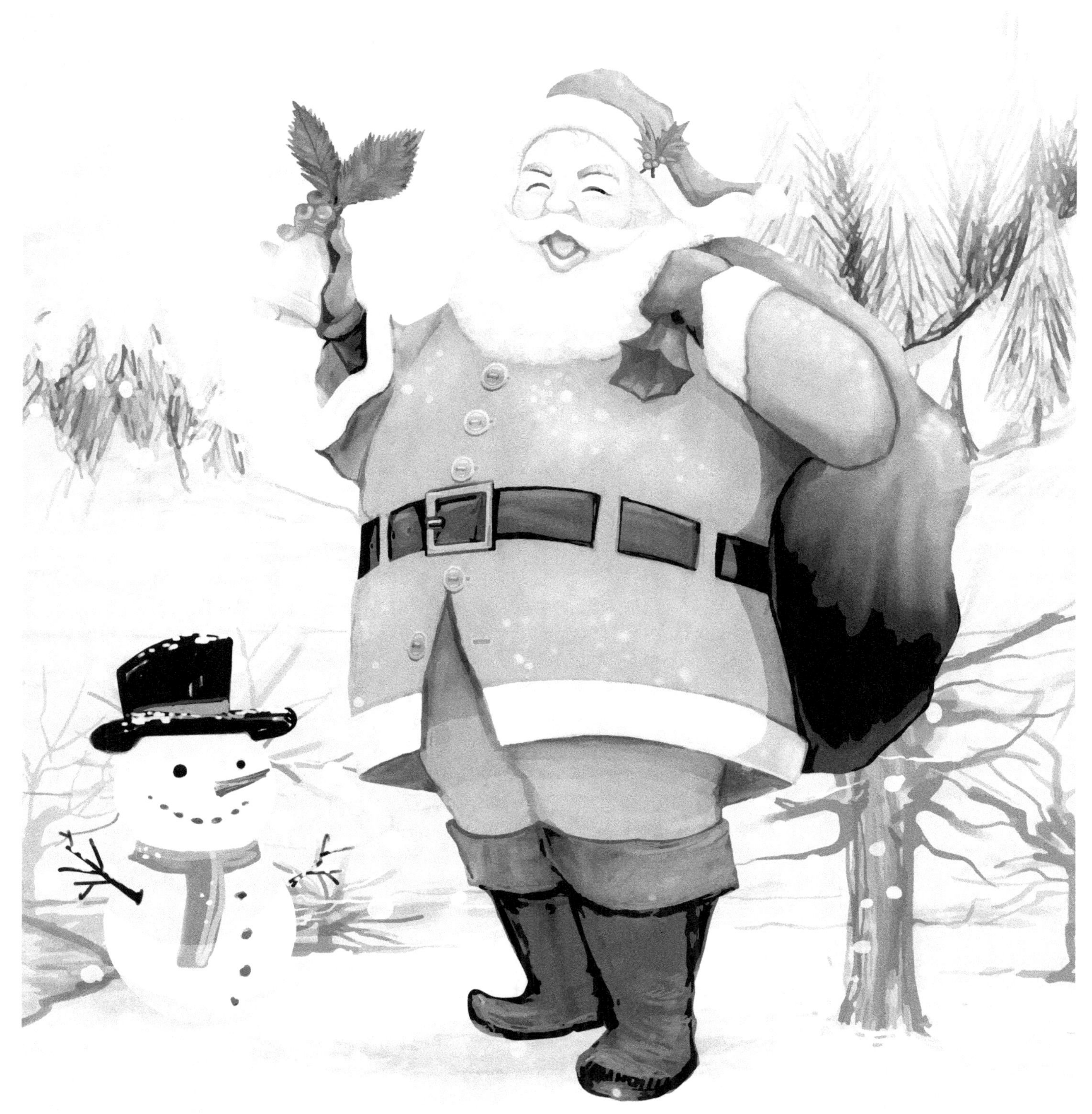

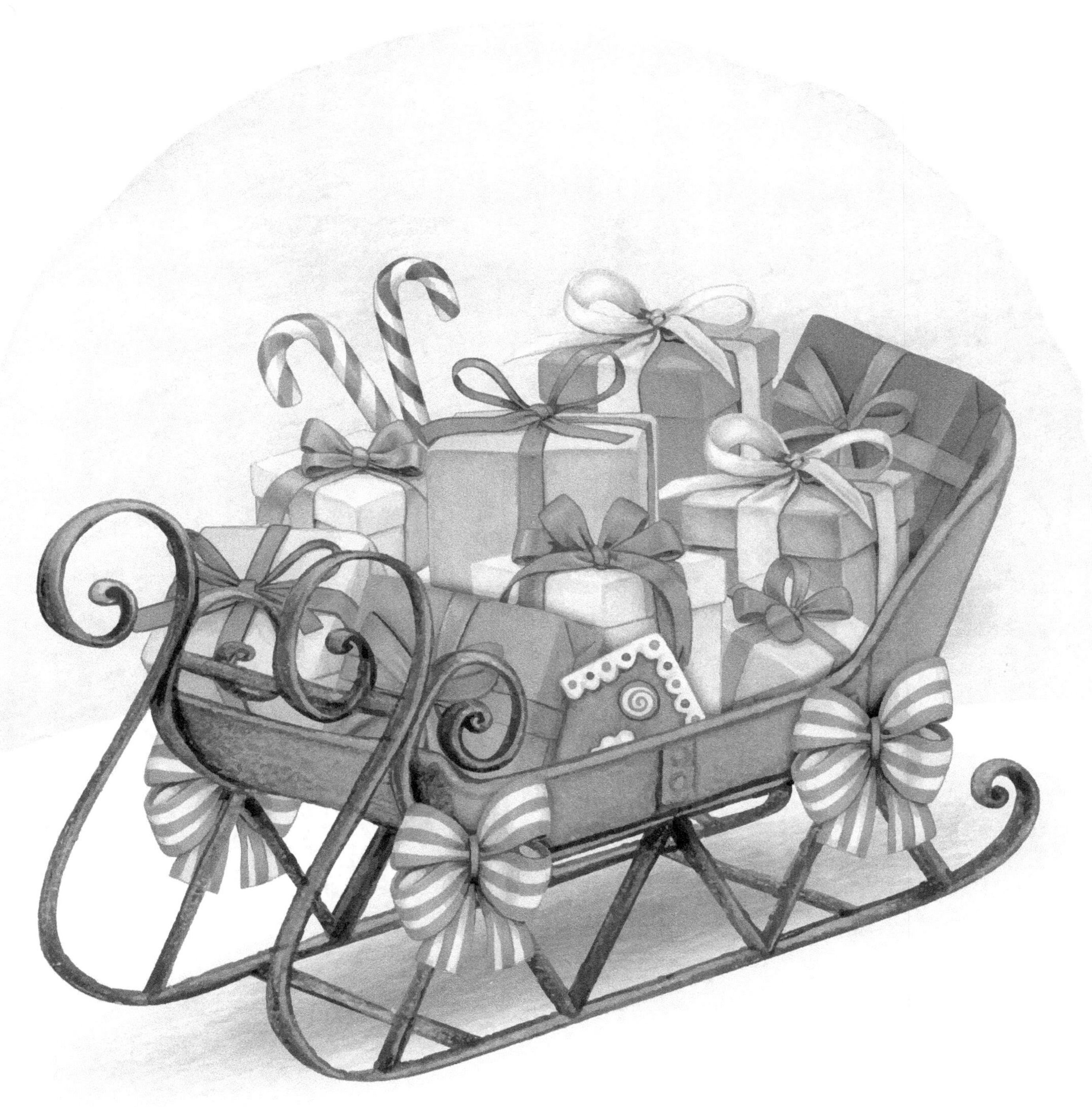

Happy New Year

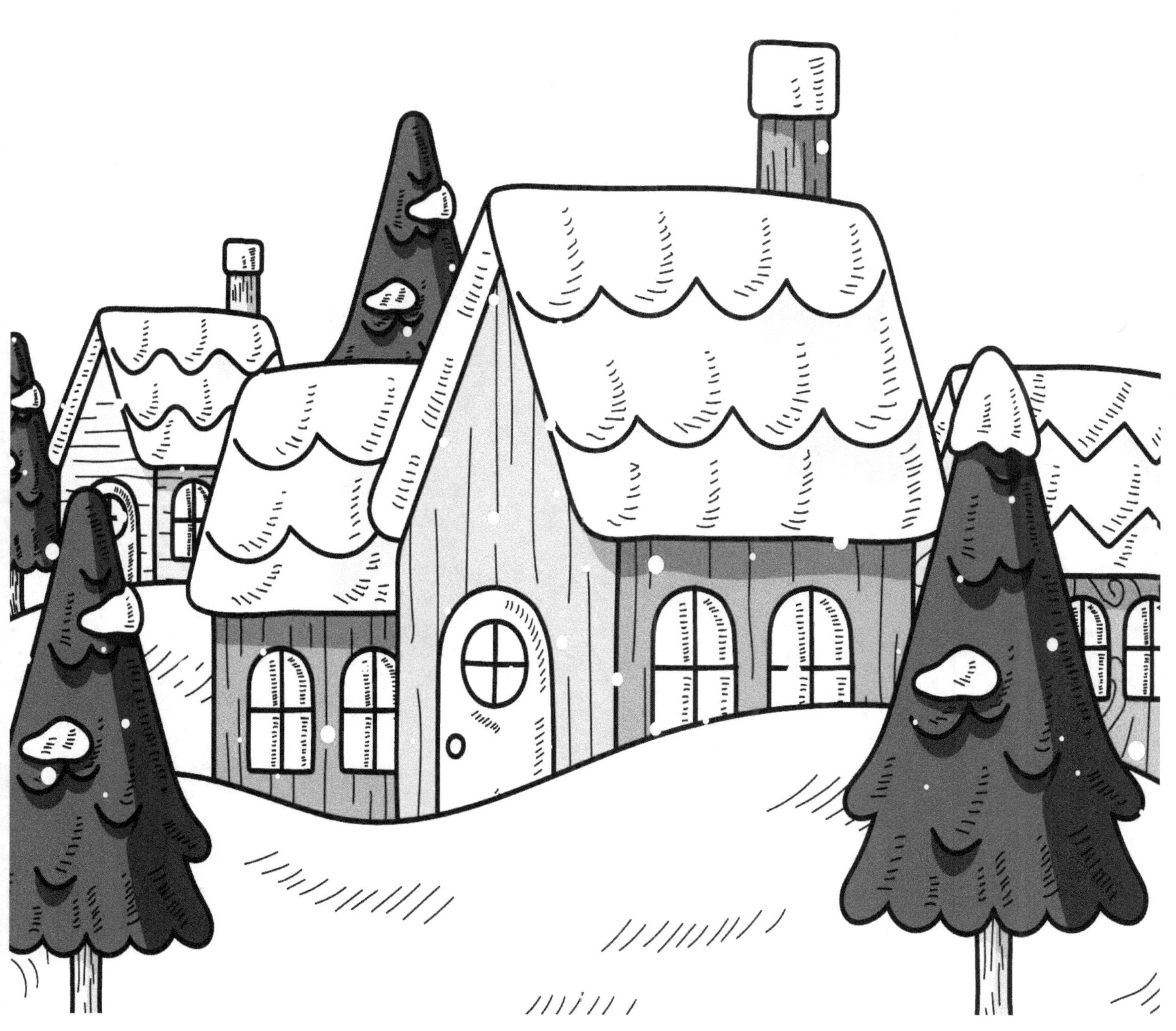
Merry Christmas

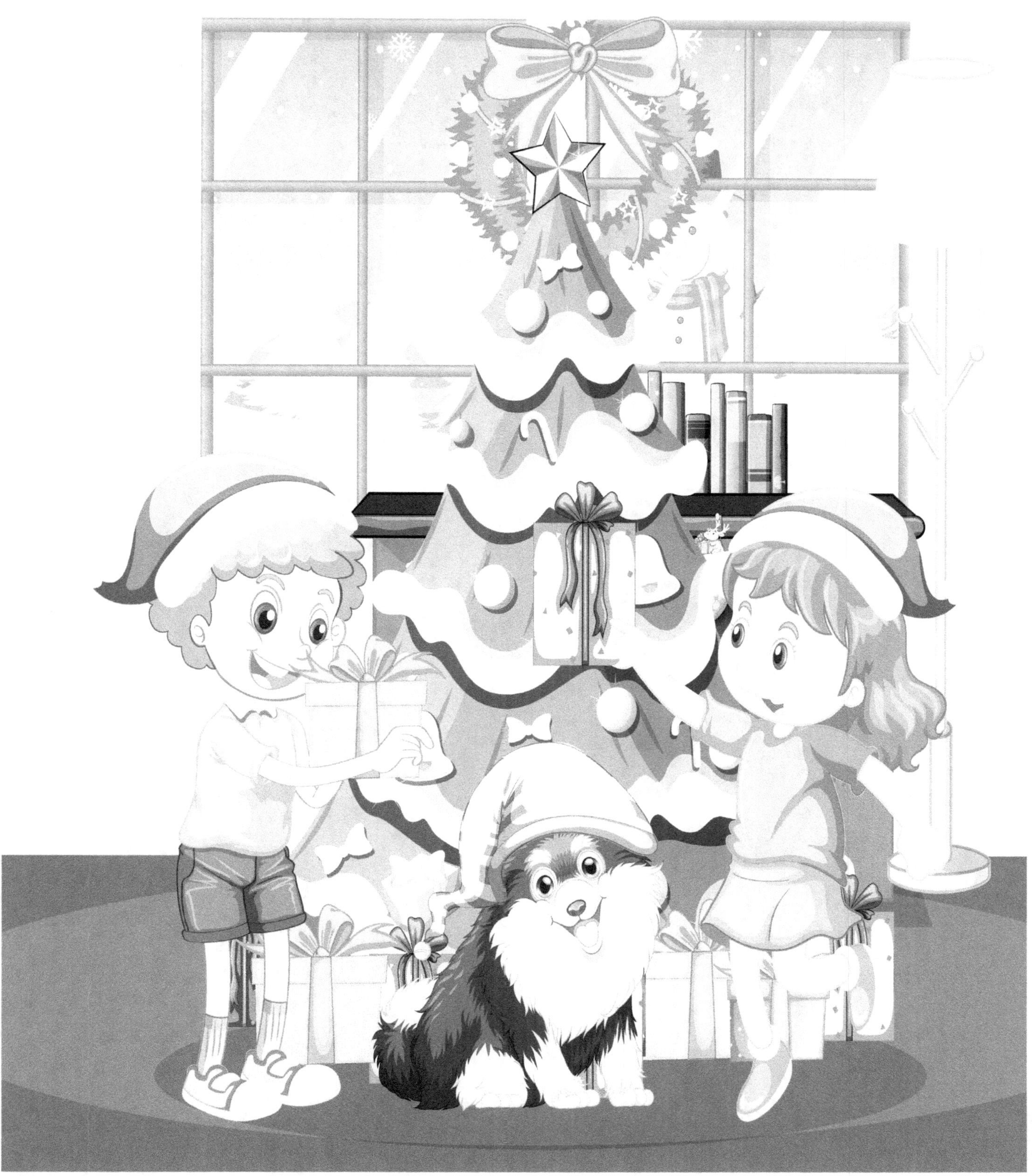

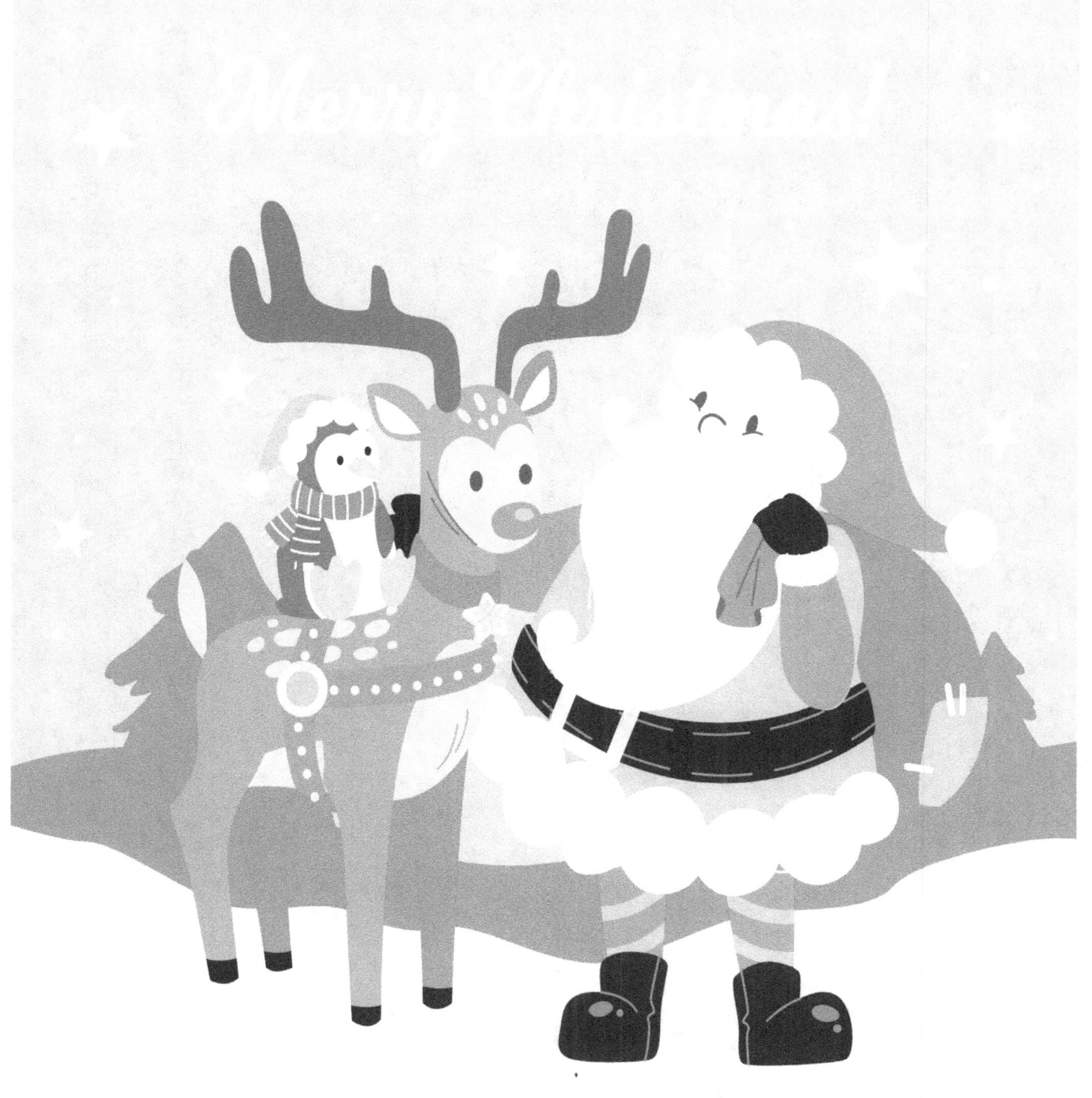

Merry Christmas!

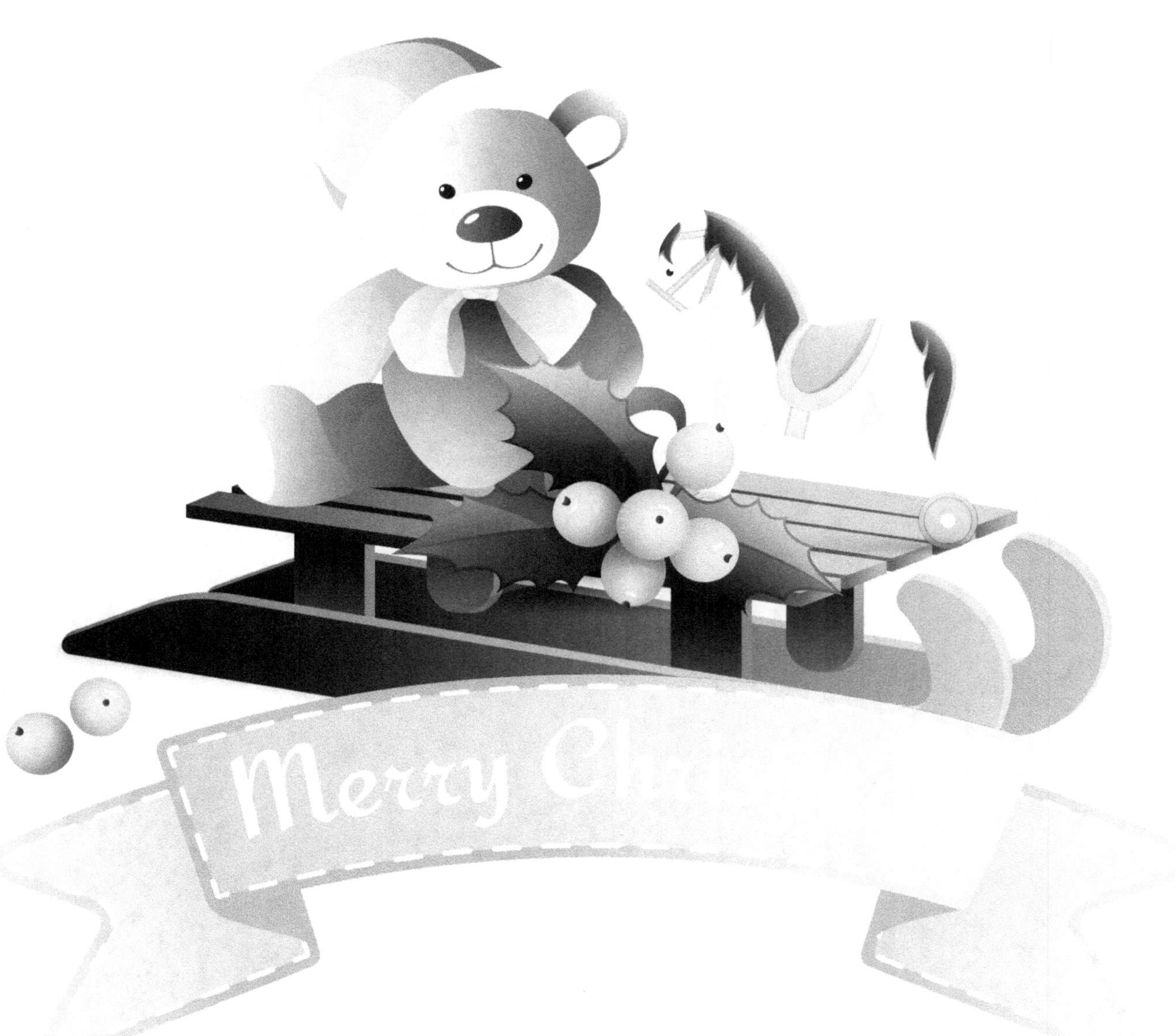
Merry Chr

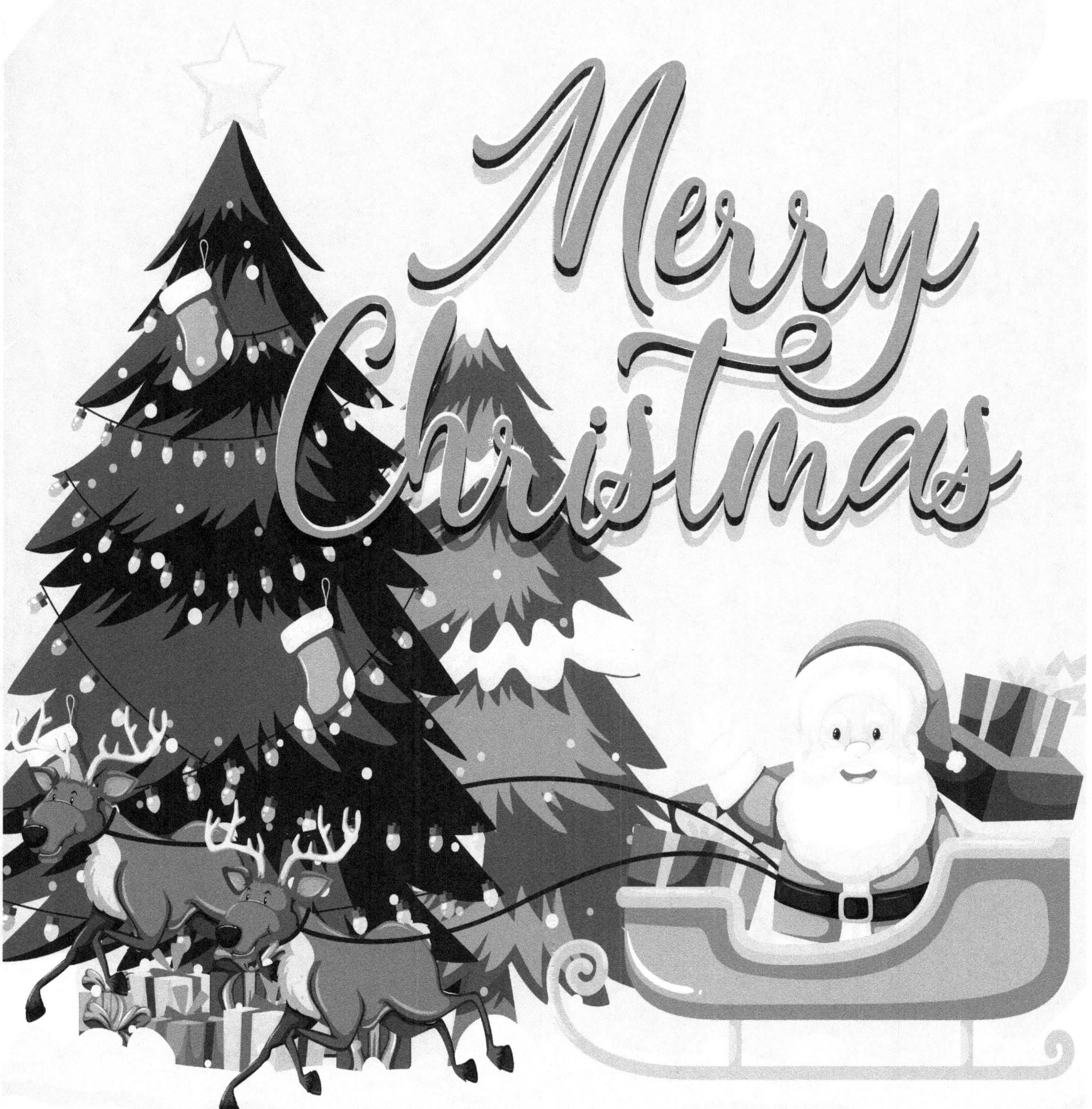
Merry Christmas

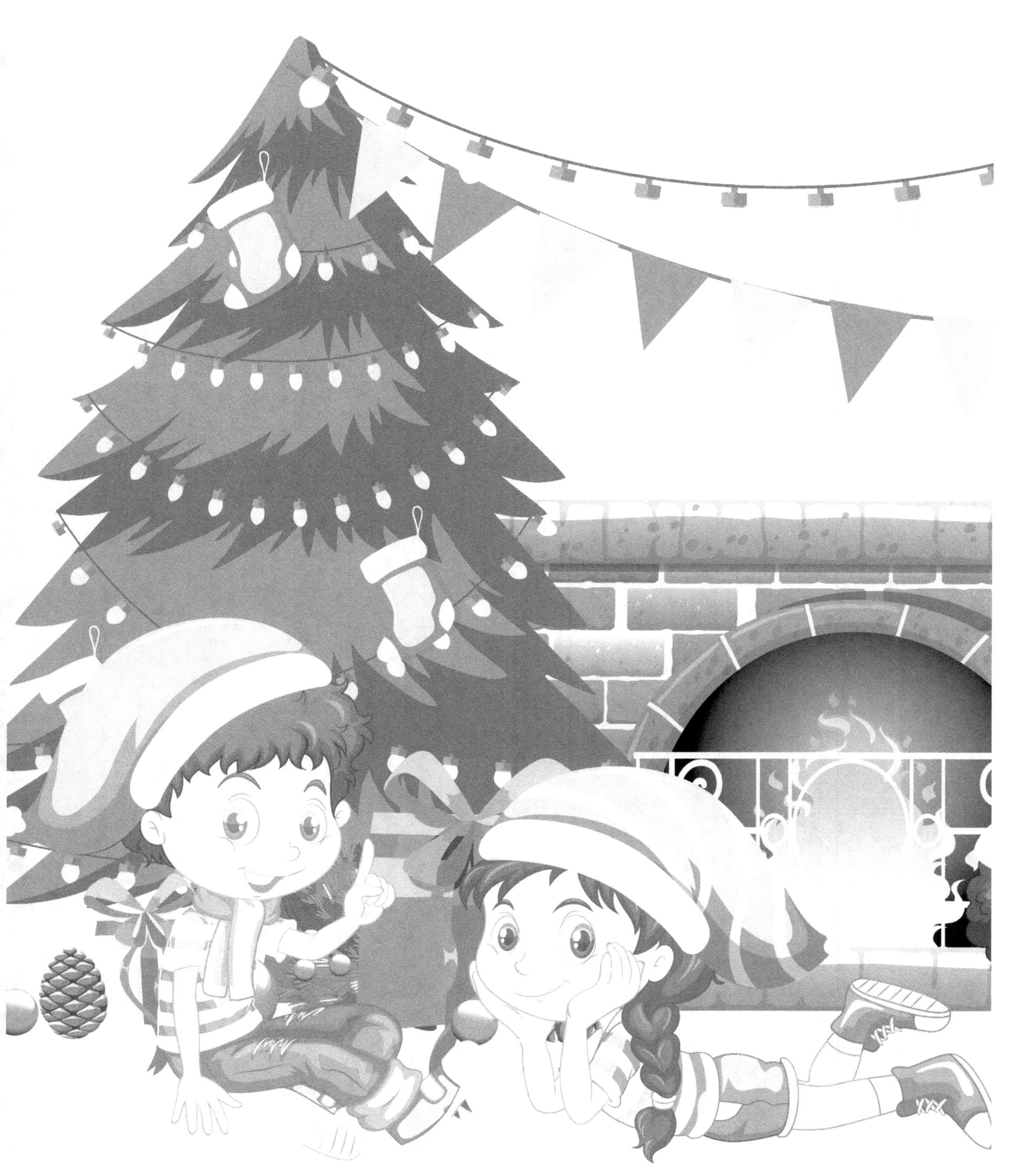

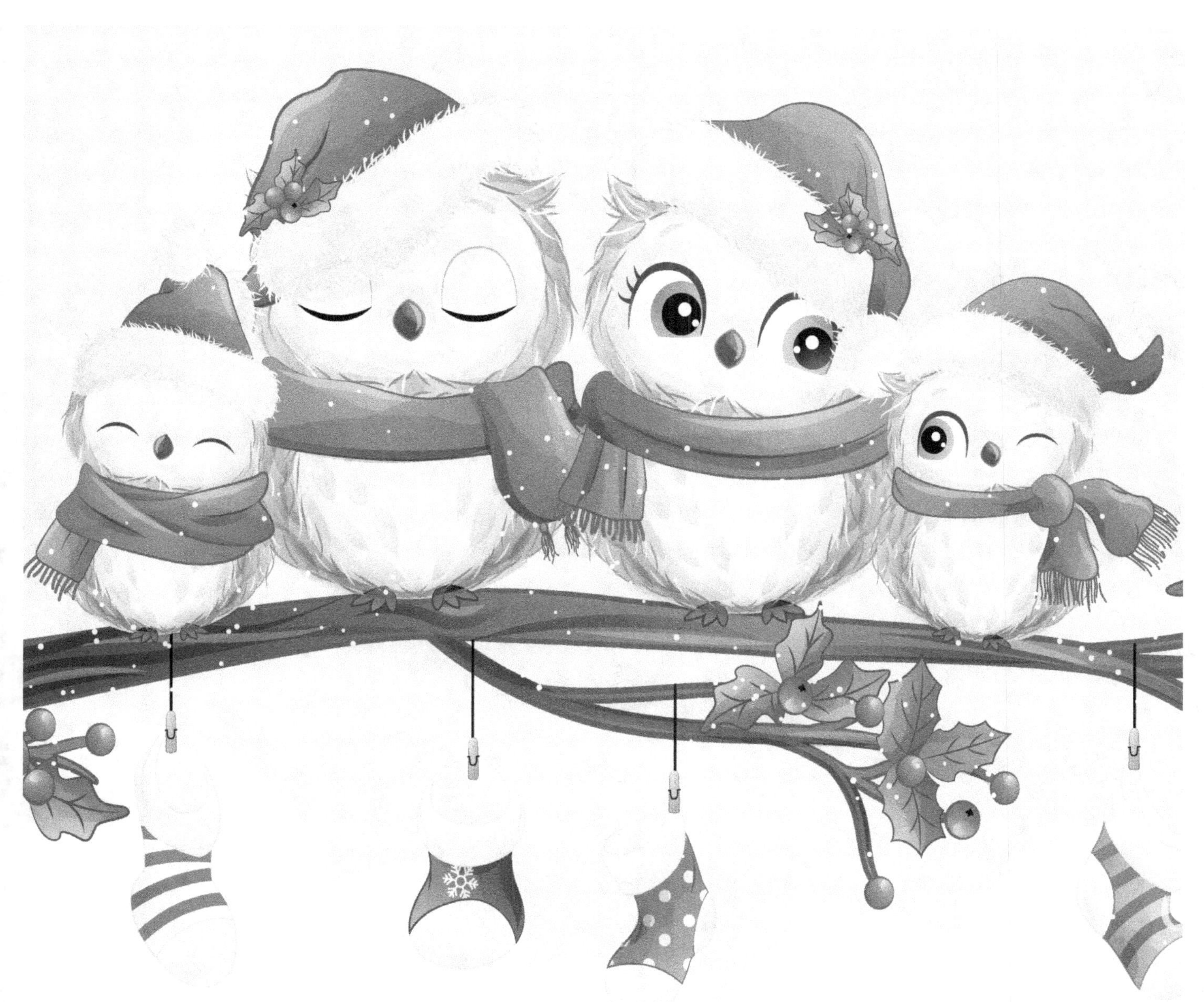

MERRY CHRISTMAS

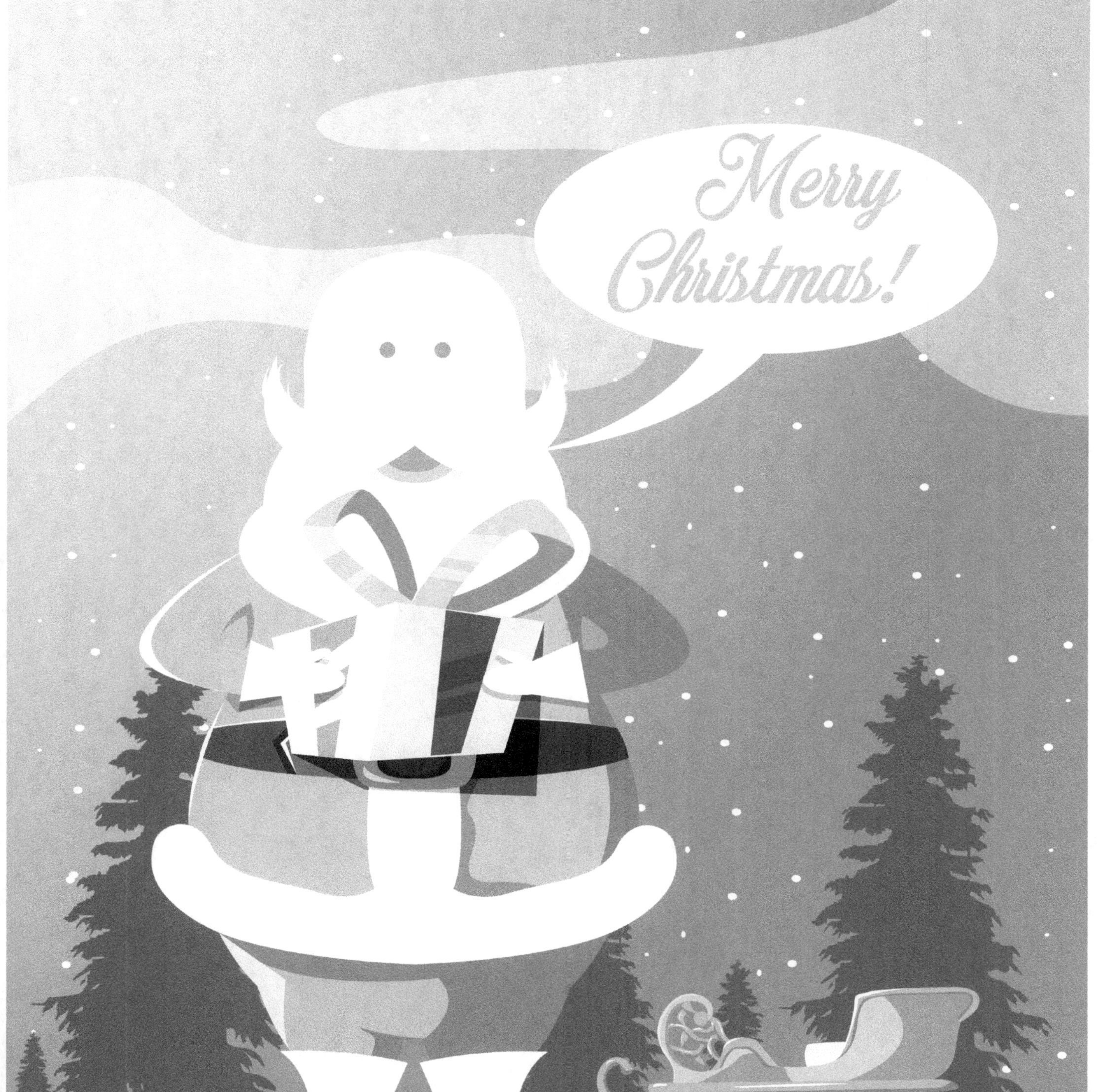

Merry Christmas!

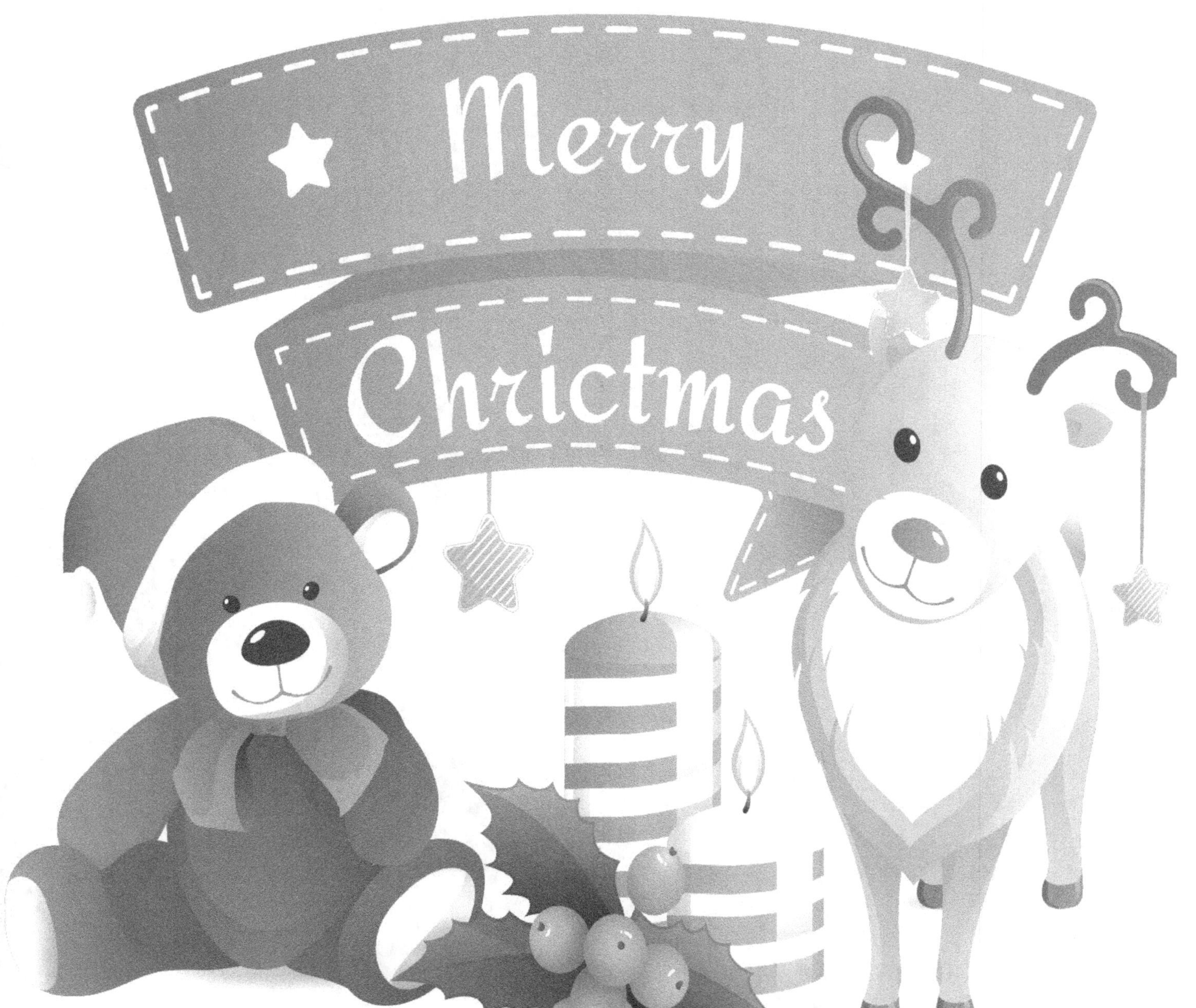
Merry
Chrictmas

Merry Christmas

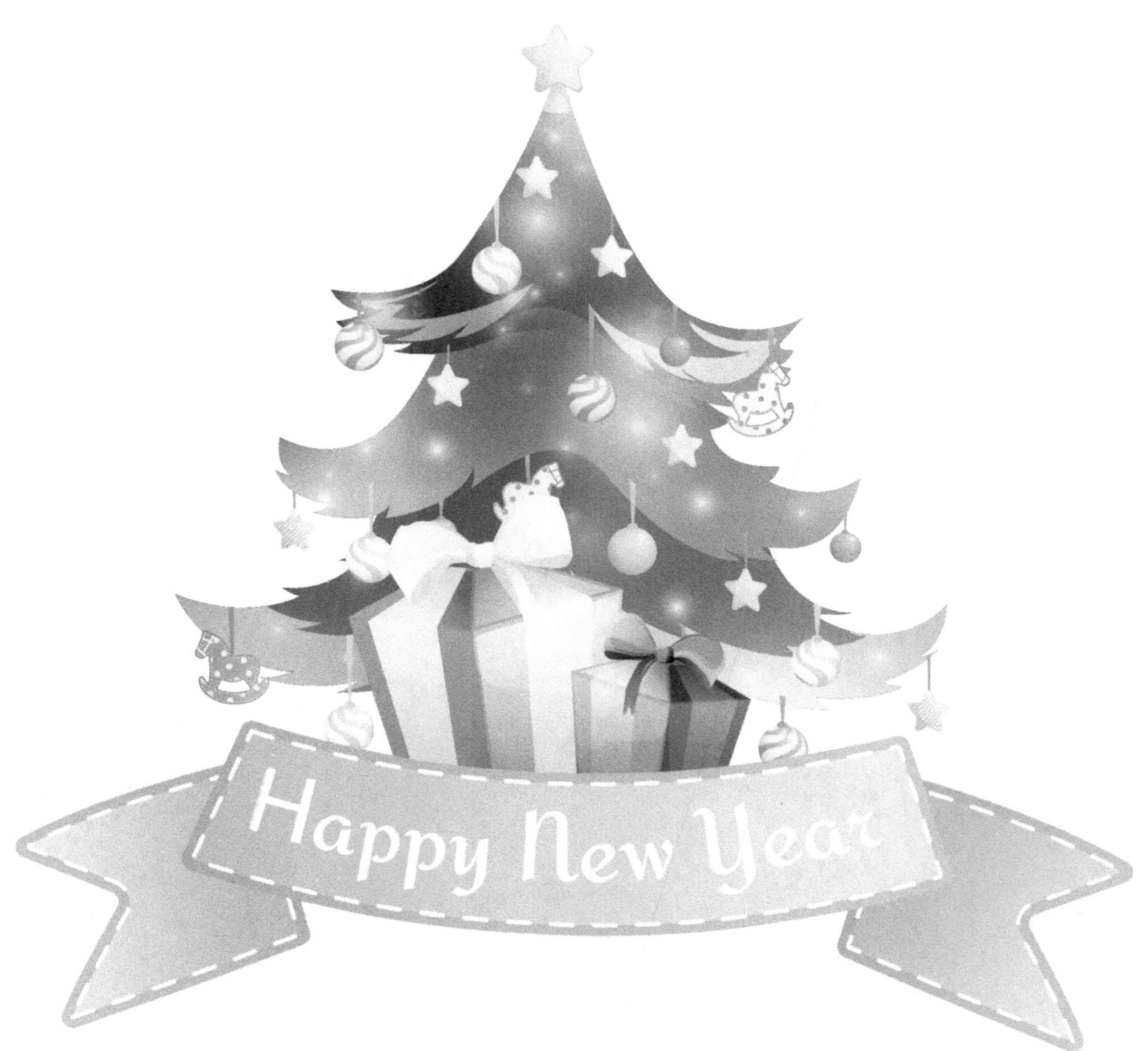
Happy New Year

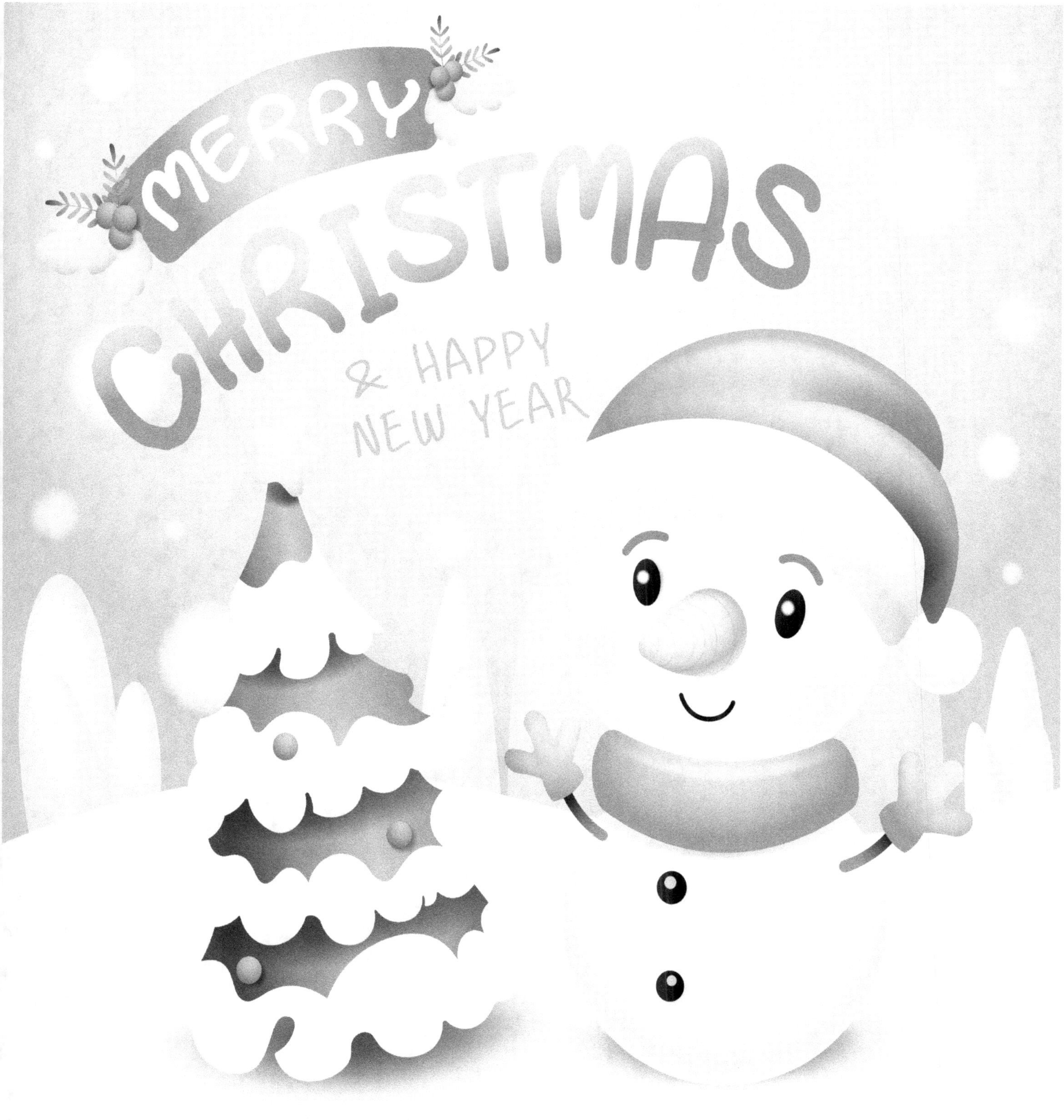

MERRY
CHRISTMAS
& HAPPY
NEW YEAR

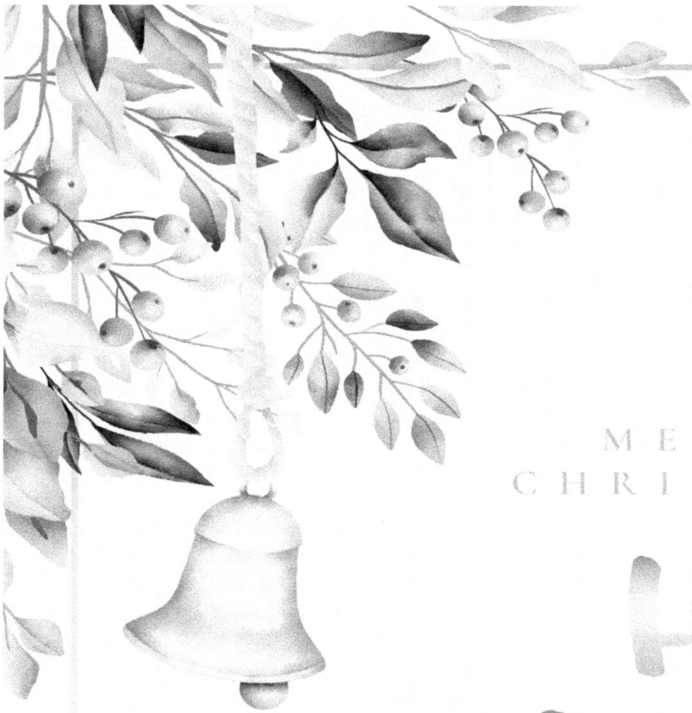

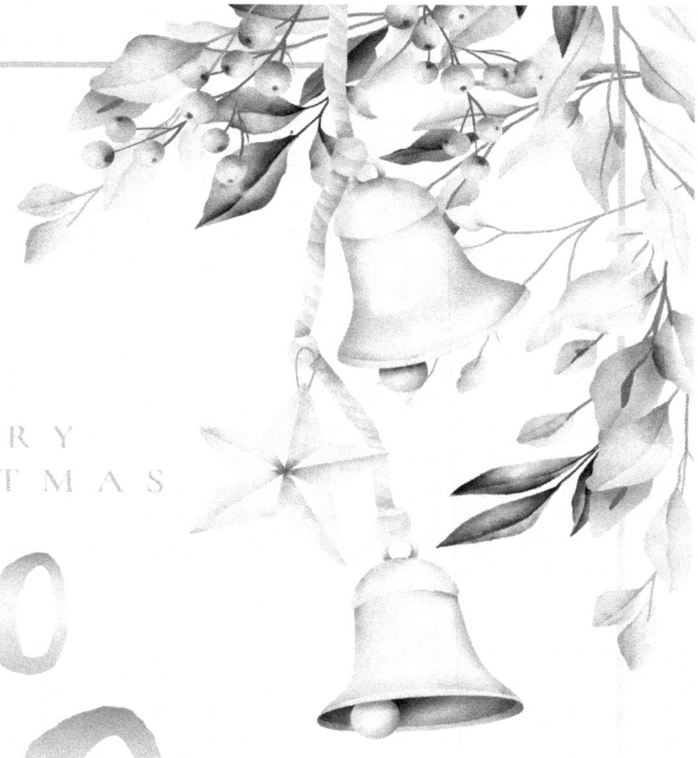

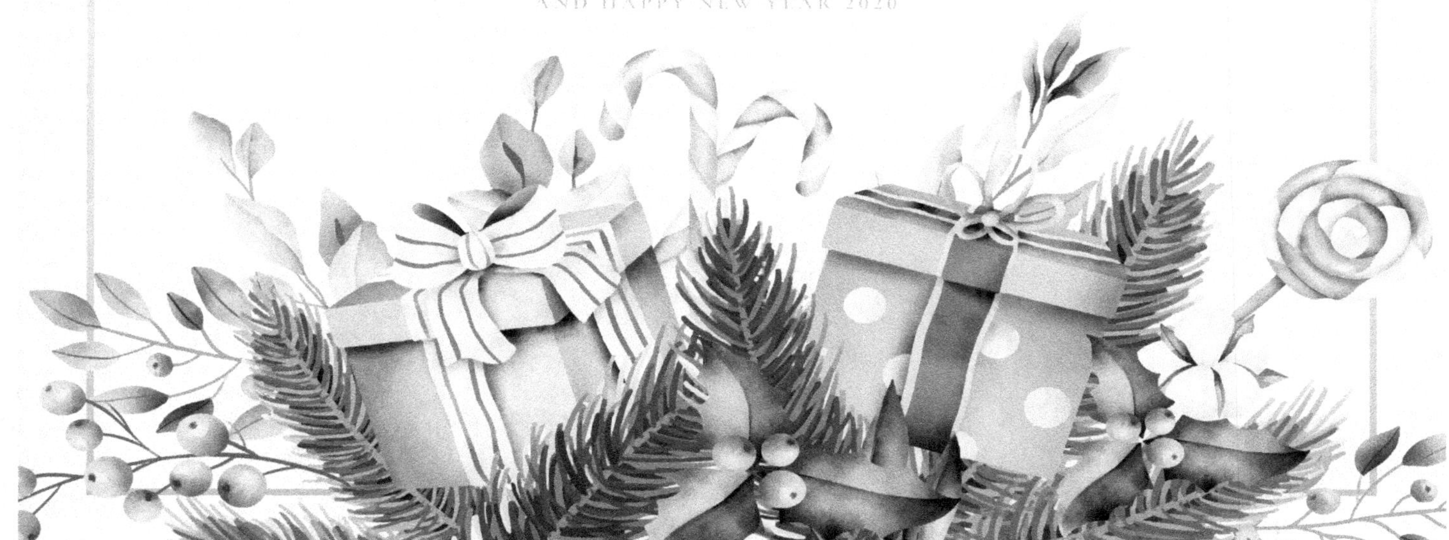

MERRY
CHRISTMAS
HO
HO
HO!
AND HAPPY NEW YEAR 2020

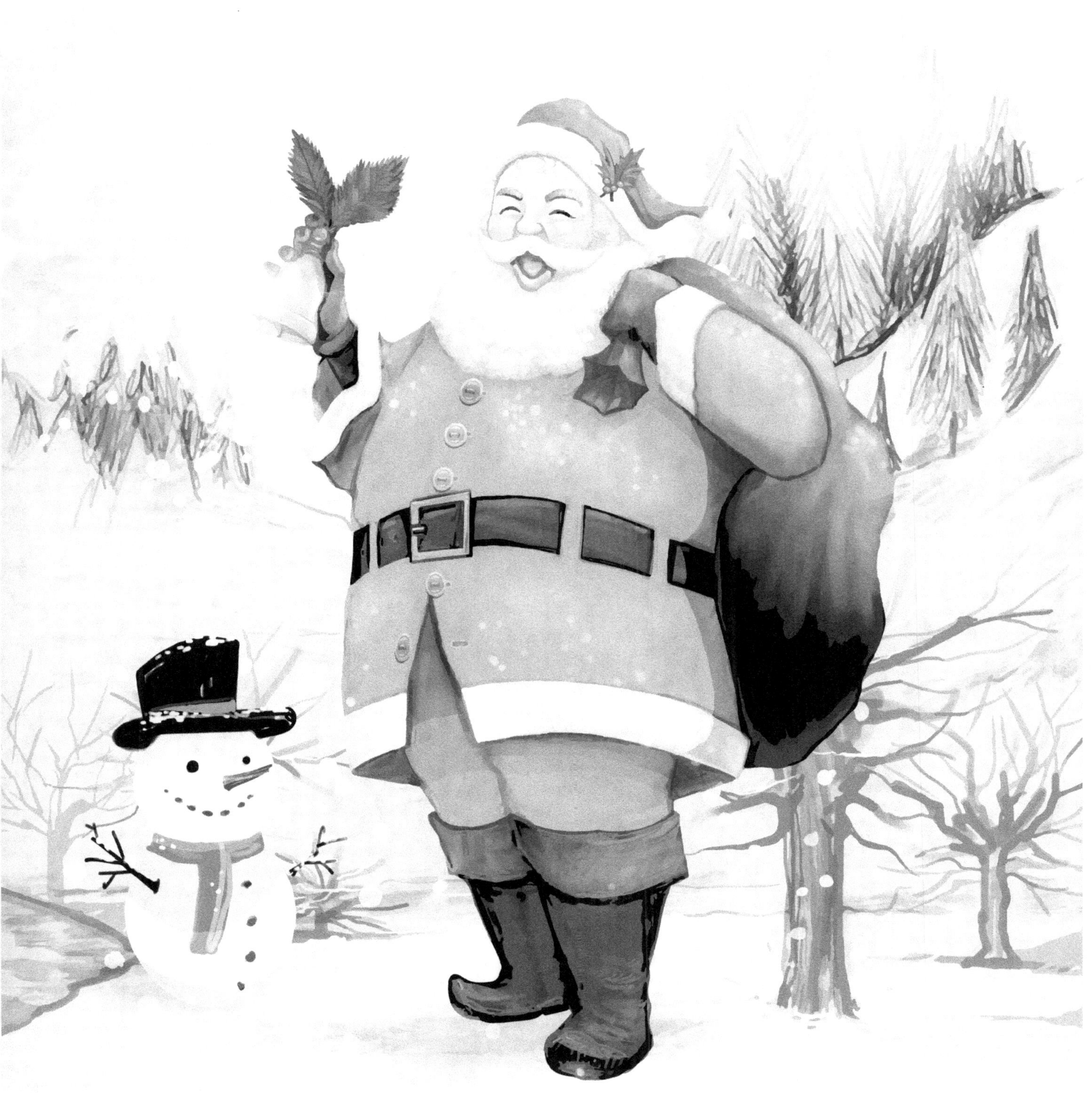

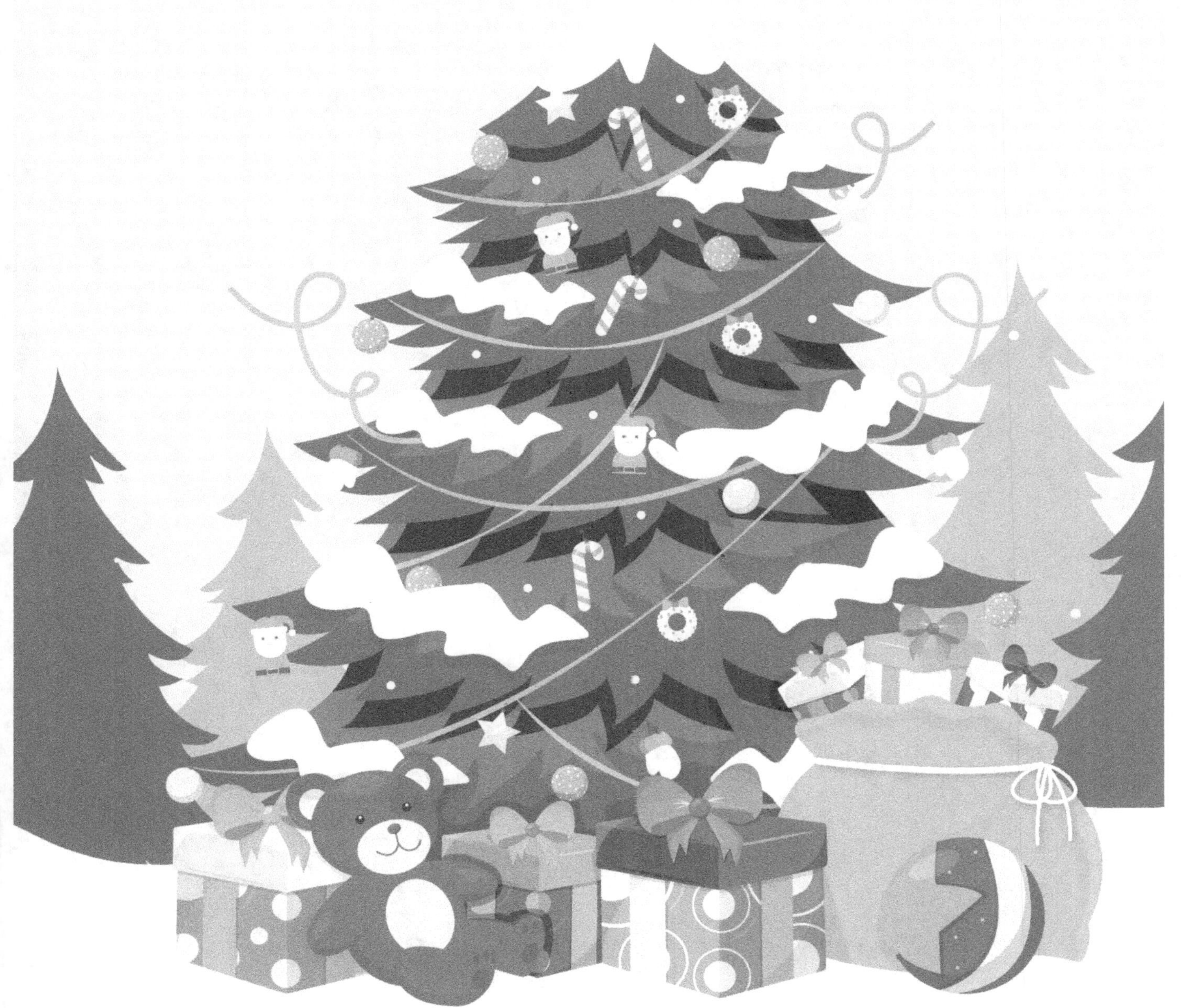
·Merry Christmas·

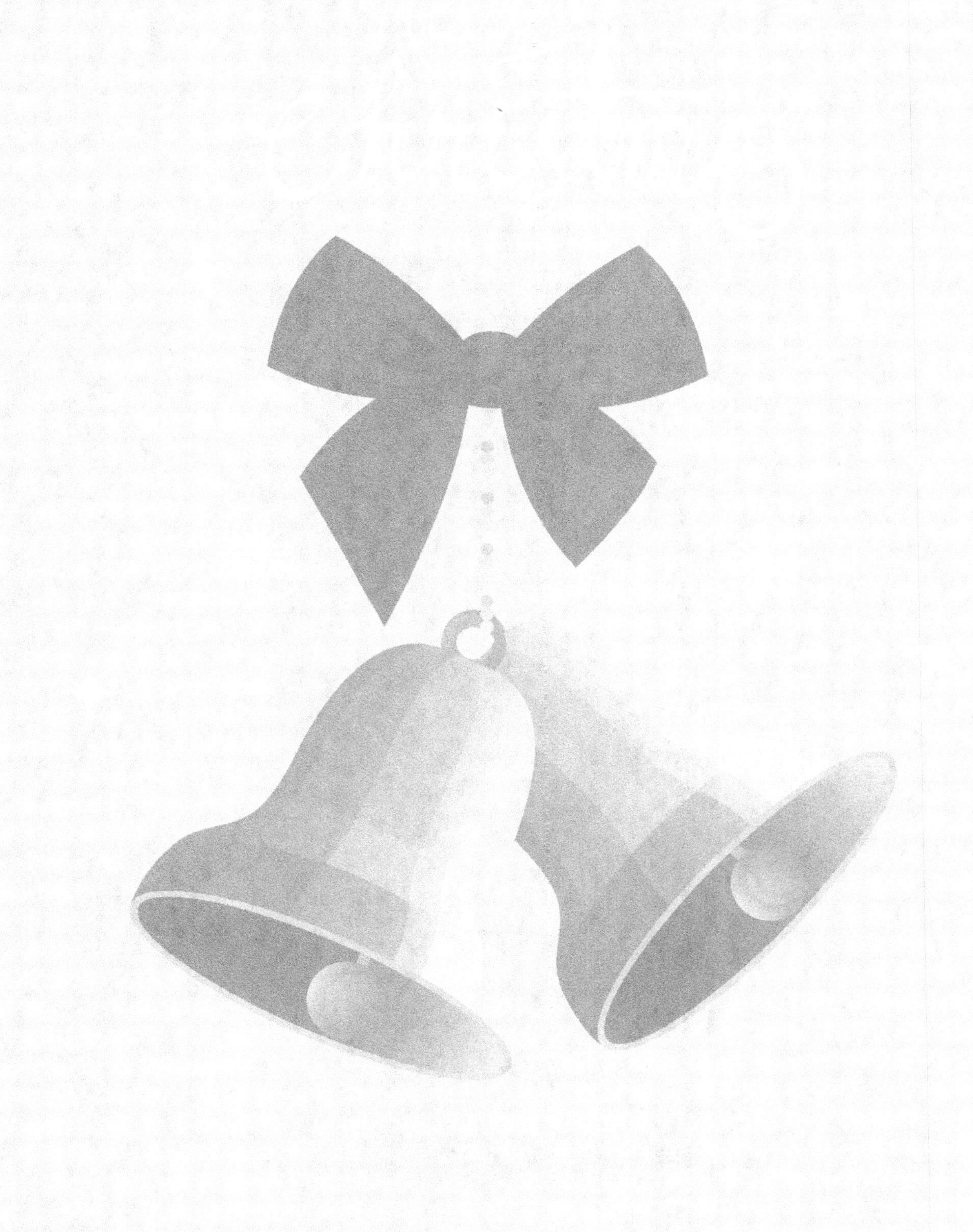

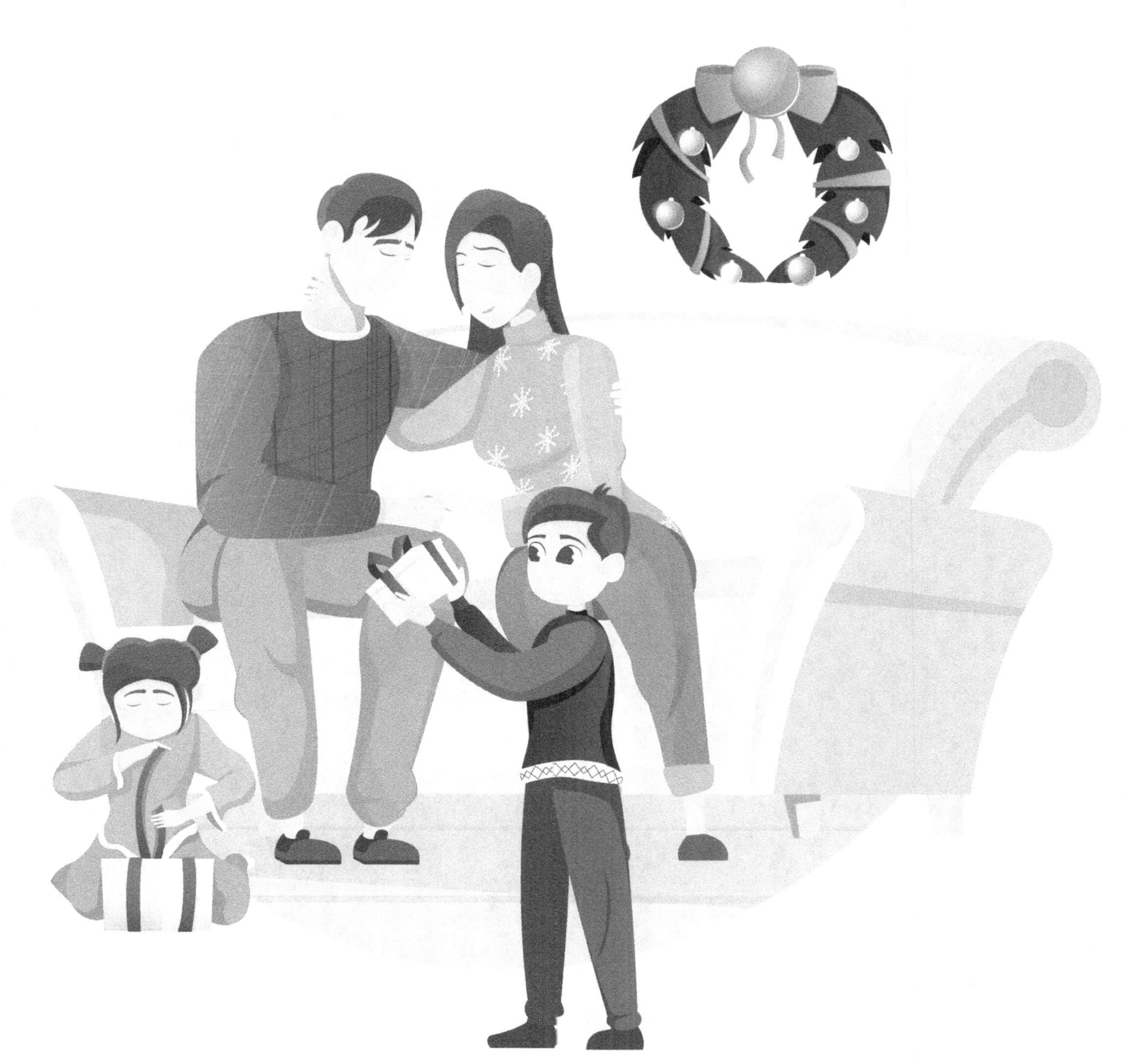

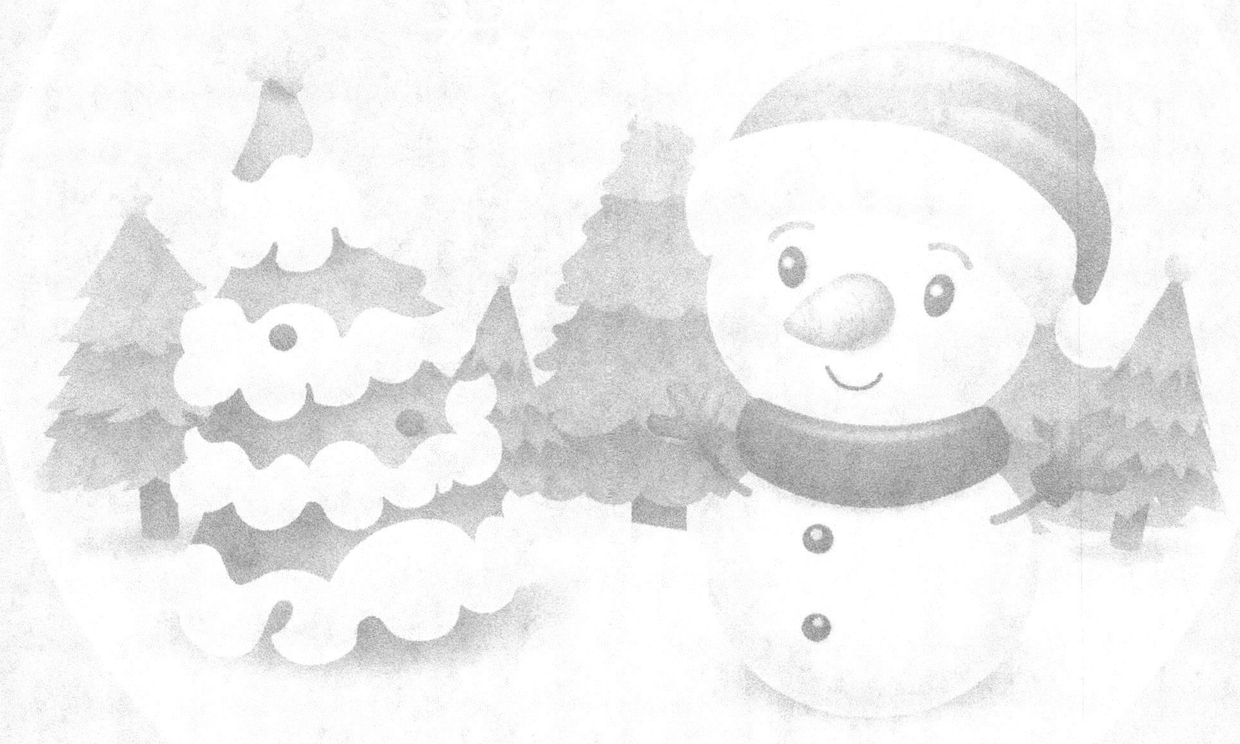
MERRY CHRISTMAS
& HAPPY NEW YEAR

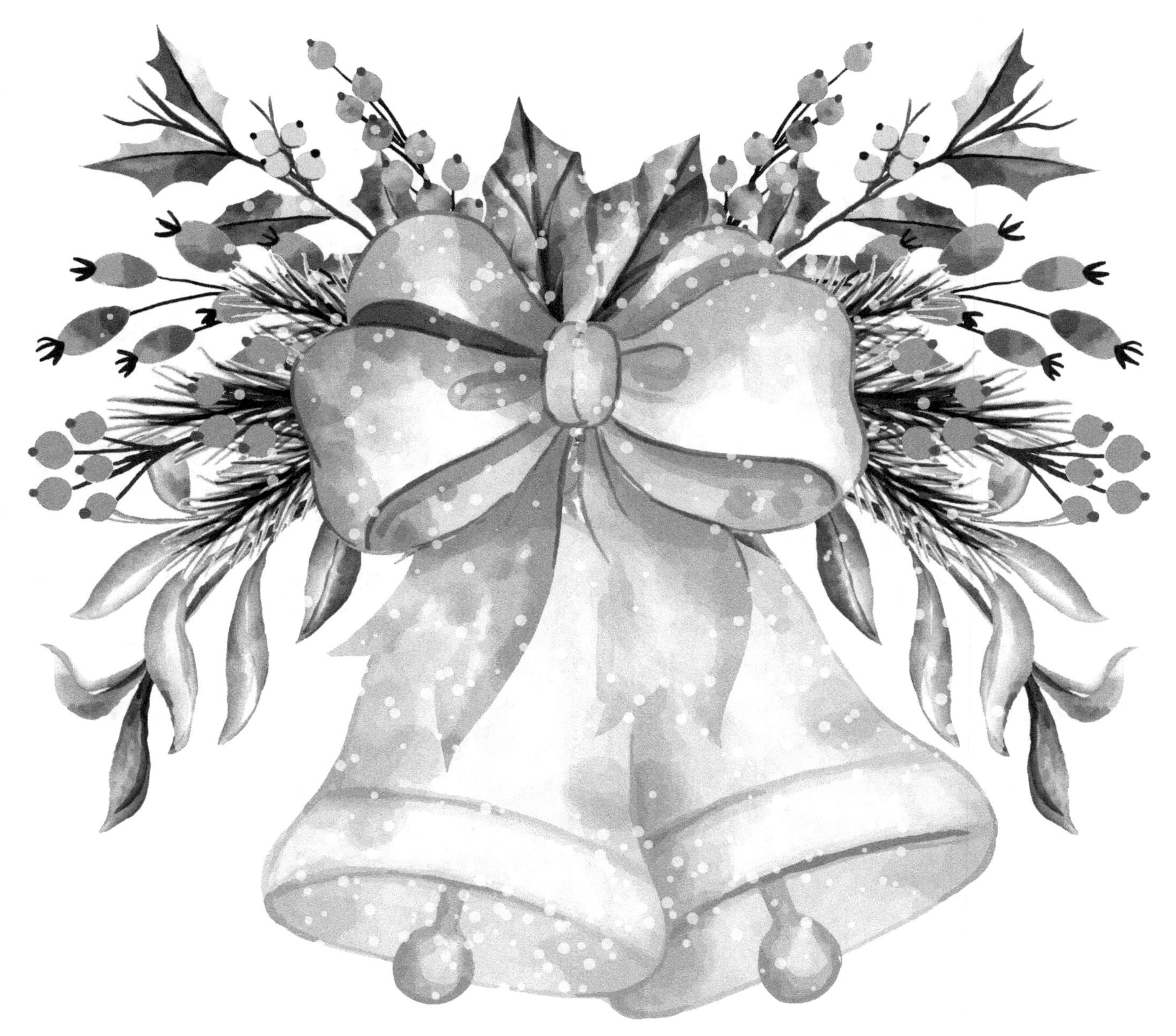

Merry Christmas

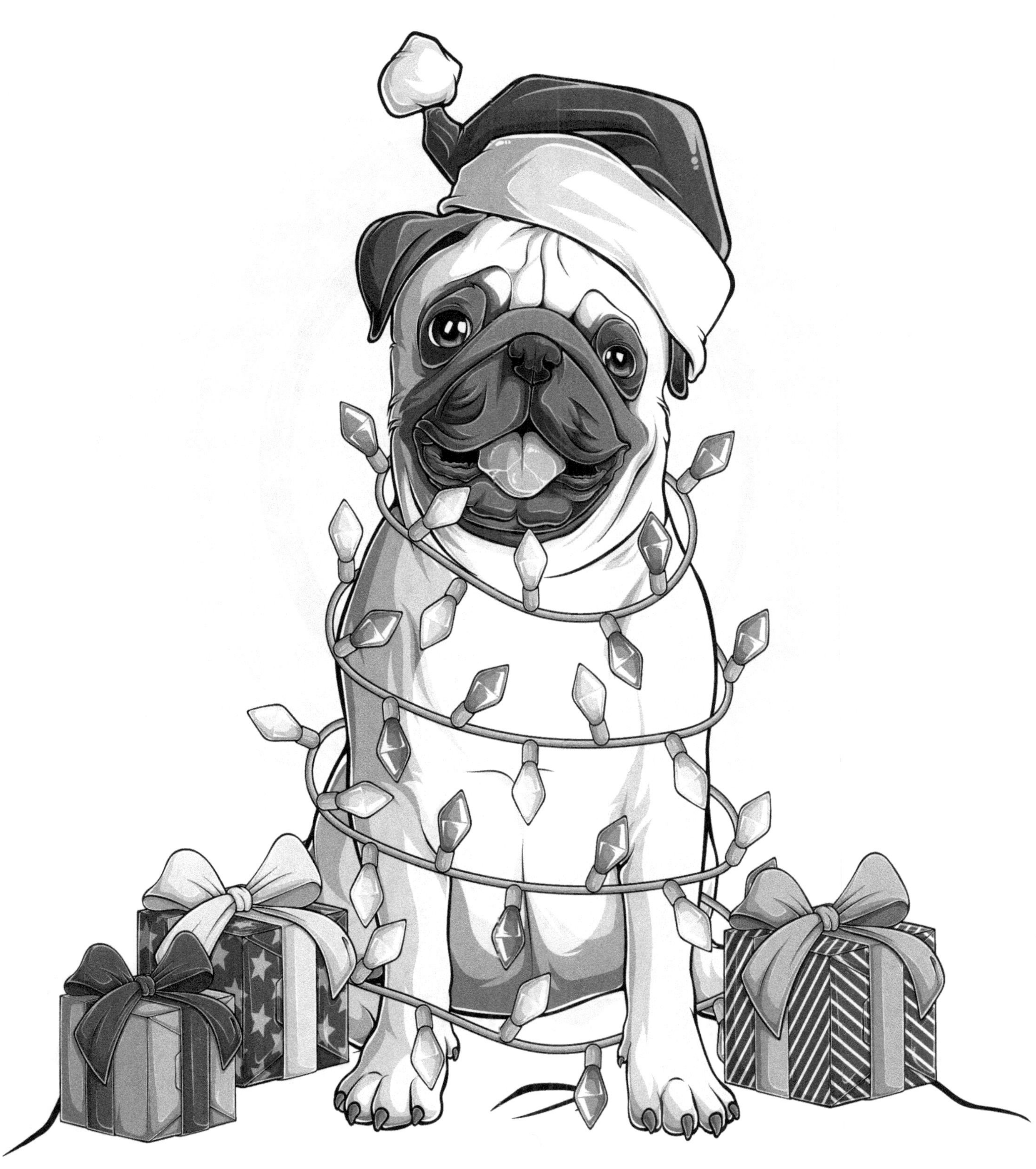

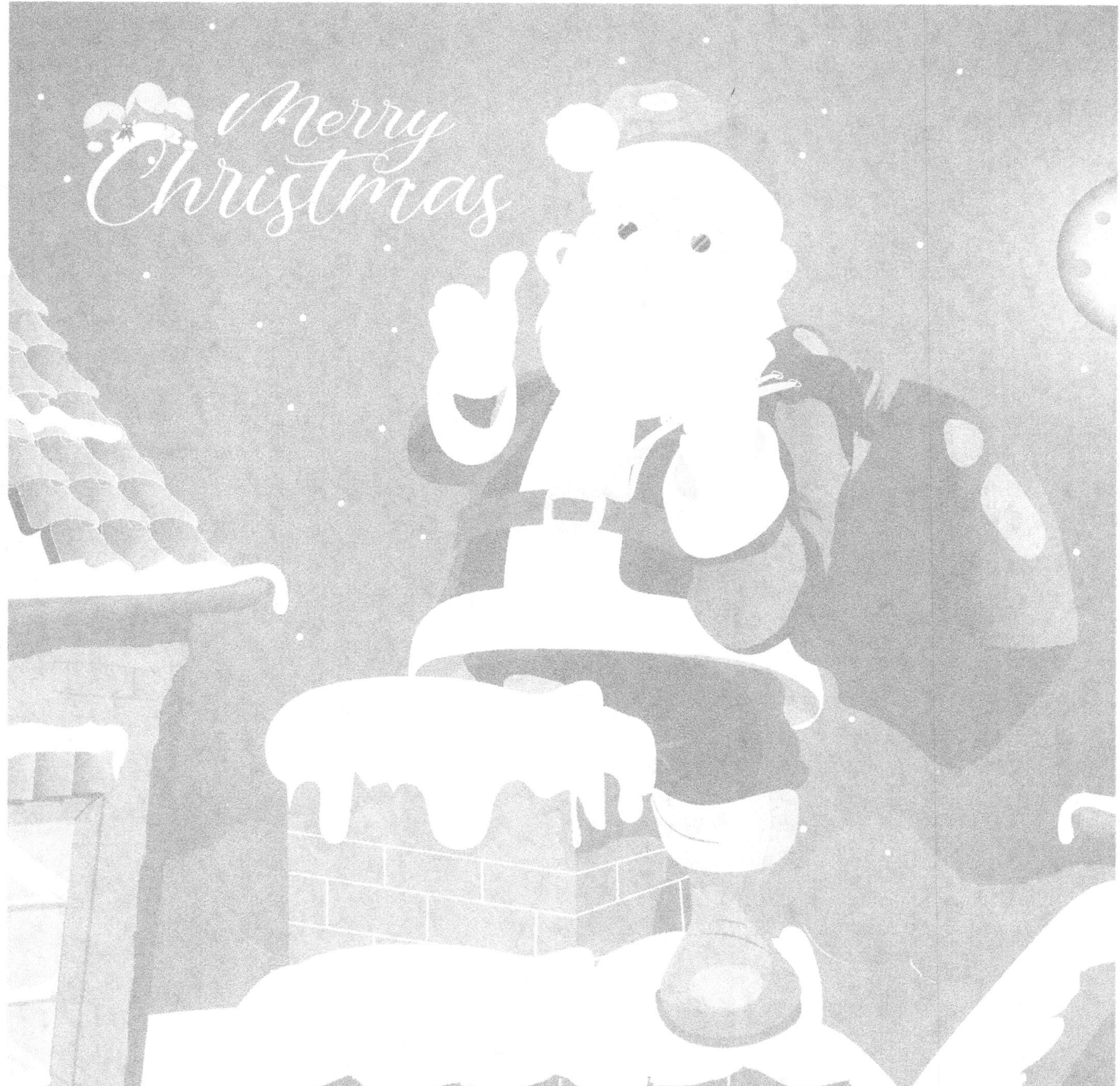
Merry
Christmas

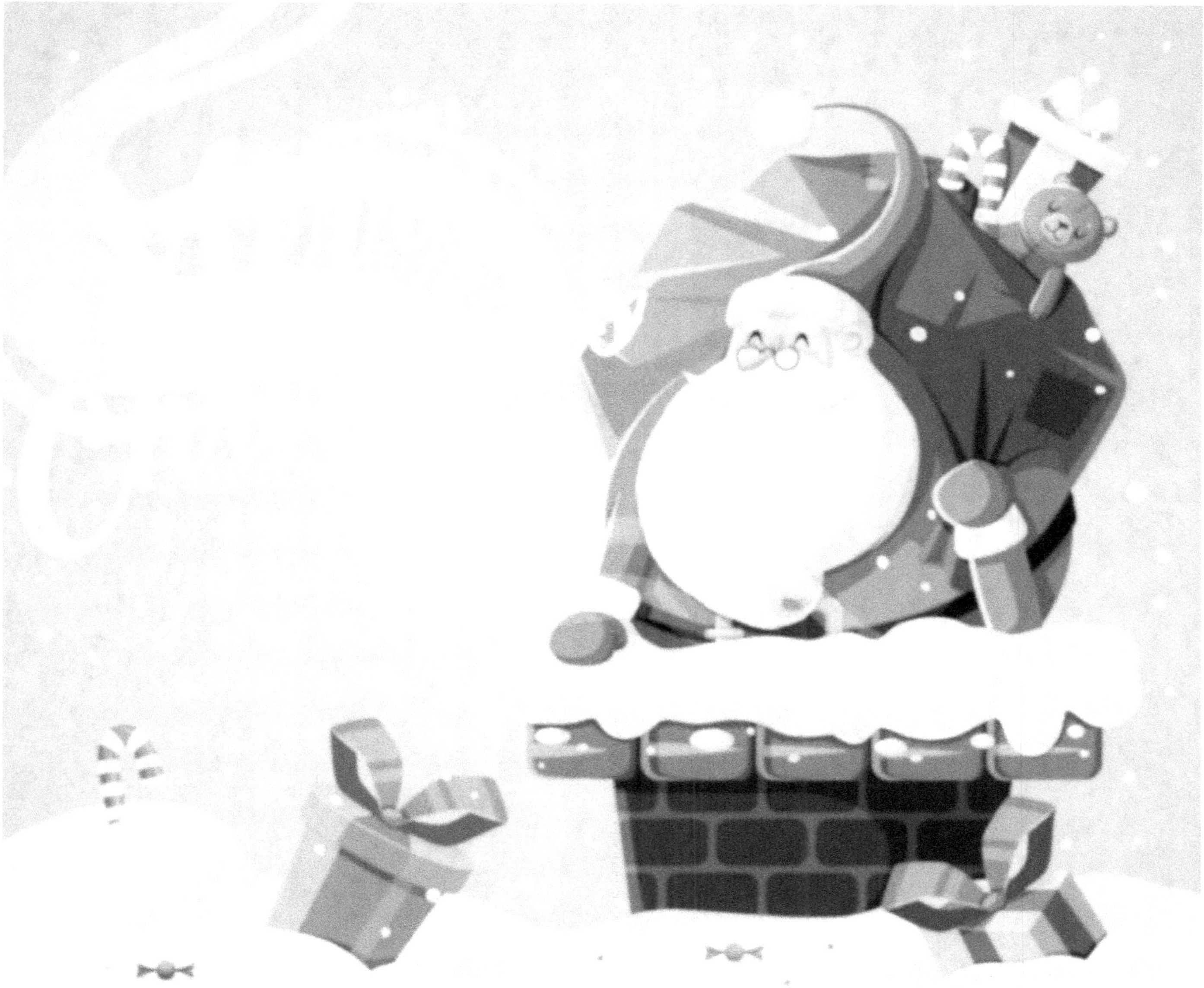

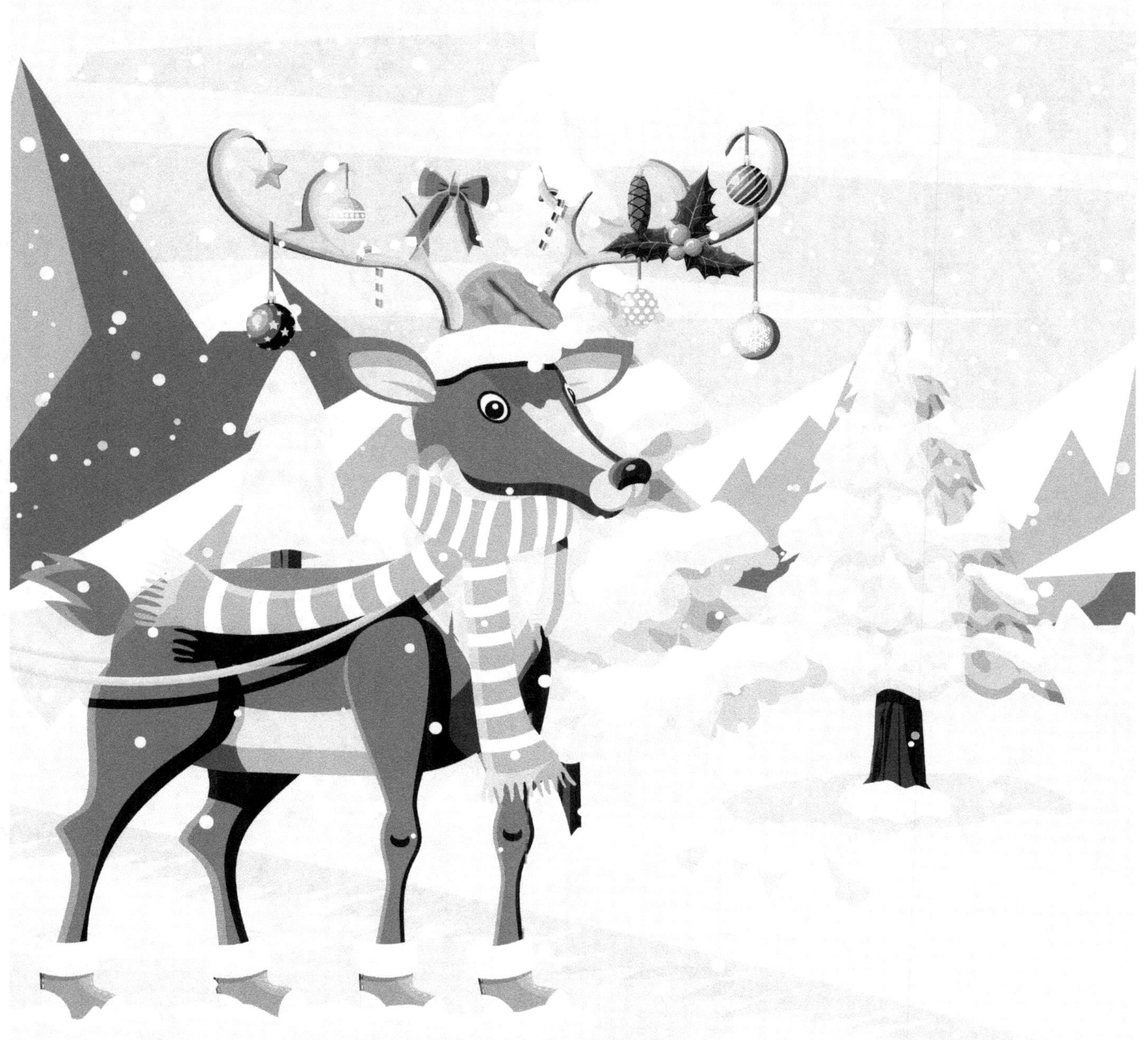

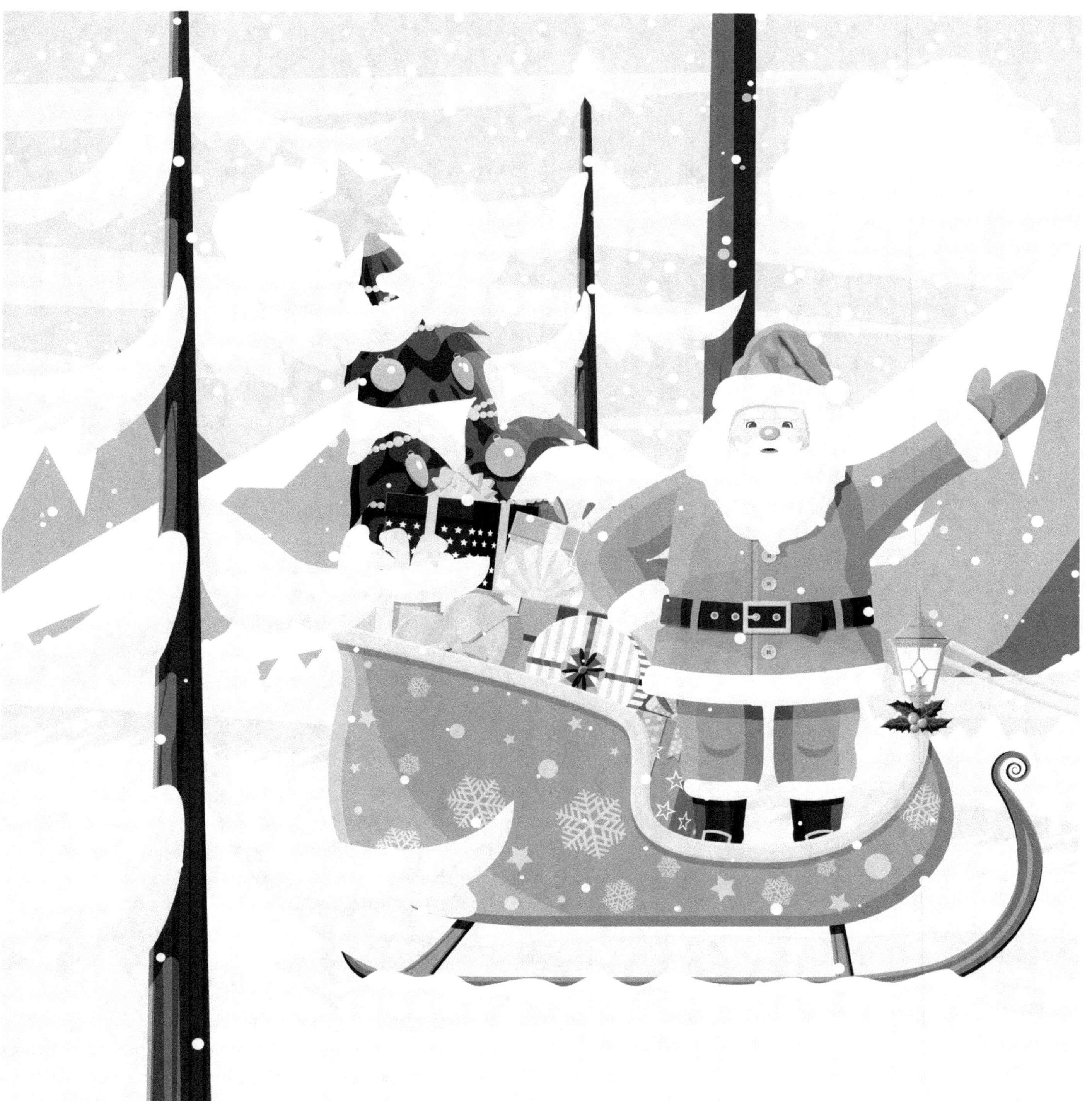

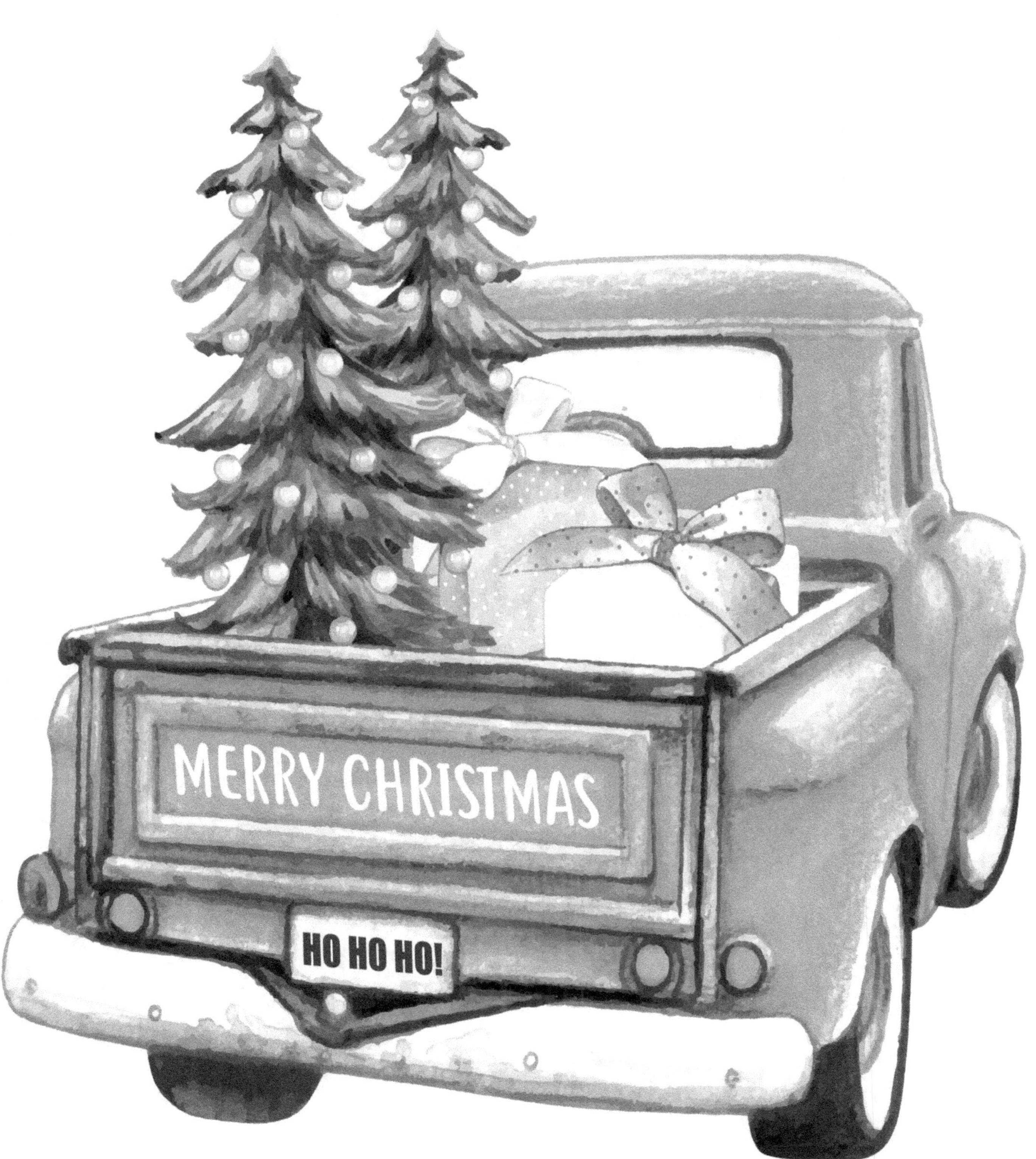

MERRY CHRISTMAS
HO HO HO!

Instagram: Tag your colored pictures with #colour_my_art for a change to get your pictures featured on our social media.

Thank you for your purchase

Laura Devon

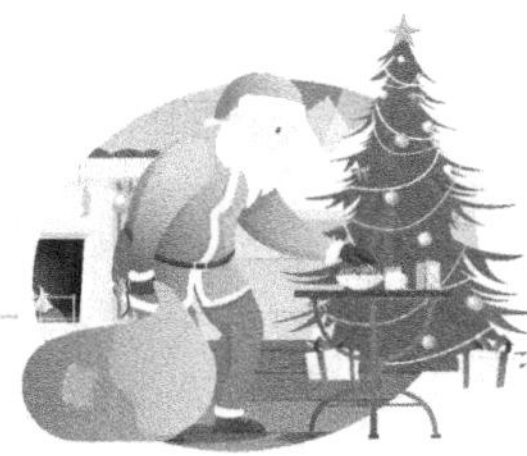

www.ingramcontent.com/pod-product-compliance
Lightning Source LLC
LaVergne TN
LVHW060415200726
843506LV00007B/452